T3-BNJ-762

OMNIVM LVX CIVIVM

Books by Ignazio Silone

The School for Dictators

Translated from the Italian by William Weaver

New York   Atheneum   1963

THE
SCHOOL
FOR
DICTATORS

IGNAZIO
SILONE

With a Preface by the Author to the New Edition

Preface to the New Edition

THIS BOOK, first published in 1939, was originally written in the context of the situation then prevailing, and while it also dealt with principles and problems of a general nature, it was primarily concerned with the immediate need of defending democracy. Thus, while offering a critique of the Fascist and Nazi ideologies, it also attempted to expose their falsification of history (then enjoying a vogue which extended even beyond the immediate sphere of their hegemony) and to define the social factors which facilitate totalitarian enter-enterprises in the present age.

Since then, military defeat has rid the political scene of the macabre figures who in Italy and Germany so long encumbered it. It would nevertheless be idle to pretend that the significance of those bitter experiences has been universally grasped, and still less that dictatorships have now vanished from the earth, or that very many democrats are aware of the causes which, in contemporary society, favor the totalitarian degeneration of public life.

It seemed to me, therefore, that my little book might still serve some useful purpose. The present edition differs from that of 1939 in having been to a large extent pruned of the purely documentary parts dealing with Fascism and Nazism, at least insofar as these movements now belong to history and are no longer matters of dispute. Instead, the new edition dwells more fully and more insistently on the conditioning of political forms in present-day mass society.

It will not surprise me if some readers find the book pessimistic. Yes, there is pessimism in it, but not despair. The spirit of freedom will survive: of this I am convinced. Always, in every class of society, there will be found some free spirits, men and women who are refractory to all conditioning. There were some who, alone in the midst of degraded hordes, resisted the hypnosis, the terror, the crass stupidity, of the Hitler and Stalin regimes. How then should we not believe that wherever general conformism prevails such men will always be found? This alone, I think, will suffice to prevent human society from withering away altogether, and will enable it to bloom again as soon as new circumstances permit.

IGNAZIO SILONE
June 1963

Contents

The School for Dictators

*Quam parva sapentia
regit mundum.*

1.

*In which the author meets the
American Mr. Double You, aspiring
dictator, and his ideological adviser, the
famous Professor Pickup, who have
come to Europe in search of
Columbus's egg.*

IN MY LIFE as a writer I come across plenty of peculiar people, but few as peculiar as the two Americans I
met today here in Zurich, where I have been living
since political troubles forced me to leave my native
country.

In spite of the fact that three quarters of little
Switzerland's boundaries touch countries with totalitarian regimes (I am writing this in the spring of
1939), Zurich has remained a crossroads, always
crowded with travelers from every part of the world.
Obviously, not all these people are interesting or
discreet or worthy of confidence. Some time ago I invented a watertight excuse which enables me to refuse interviews to strangers without hurting their feelings. If they say they are interested in politics, I tell
them I now concern myself only with literature. Literary visitors get the opposite answer: the world situation being what it is, my thoughts are now completely absorbed by politics. Of course this little game
has one snag. If these words of mine happen to get
into print (and they sometimes do), they are apt to
convey an impression of mental instability which is
not altogether flattering. But that's a small price to
pay for the luxury of being left in peace.

Today, however, the invitation to meet these two

Americans reached me through the good offices of an august local figure, namely the concierge of a leading hotel, who managed to arouse my curiosity by dropping several intriguing hints about his protégés. So for once, the tables were turned on me, and it was I who looked forward to the meeting. "Your guests needn't take the trouble of coming to my place," I told the concierge, "I'll be at the hotel at the time you say."

The hotel is set on the summit of one of the wooded hills that look down on the city. To reach it from my house I had to walk along a short stretch of road which affords a broad and radiant view of the lake and the Glaron Alps. The season was unusually mild. Apparently there hadn't been such an idyllic spring since 1914. The sense of calm in the air today was possibly intensified by the conclusion reached at a seminar of Swiss astrologists and published in the morning paper. The astrologists declared that any fear of a European war in the coming years was absolutely groundless. Astrology, along with architecture and psychoanalysis, is one of the disciplines which flourish in this city.

"I am Professor Pickup," an elderly gentleman said, approaching me in the entrance hall of the hotel. "P-I-C-K-U-P, Pickup, in person."

"The famous inventor of pantautology?" I couldn't help asking, just to be sure.

"That's right." And by way of confirmation he repeated the basic tenet of his science: "Everyone is himself and can be nothing else but himself."

"However," he went on to say, "I didn't really invent anything. Mustn't deck myself with borrowed plumes. If you come to think of it, the entire history of philosophical theories is nothing but a collection of tautologies, in one disguise or another. My only merit is that I call a spade a spade."

"No small merit, these days. How do your colleagues treat you?"

"In a foolishly liberal manner. They've offered me a chair in a good university."

"Isn't that enough for you?"

"If it were only a question of my humble self, I could even be quite content. But I'm convinced that pantautology has all the prerequisites for becoming the official, obligatory doctrine of the State."

The Professor was dressed in black, like a parson, and even his voice resembled a preacher's. His flowing mane of corn-yellow hair gave him an impressive but inoffensive appearance, like a vegetarian lion.

"This way, please," he said to me.

"Isn't your friend with you?" I asked.

"You'll meet him shortly. But please don't mention his name, not even in his presence, and never, of course, to outsiders. He's traveling incognito, to be able to move more freely and to avoid any bother. His pseudonym is Mr. Double You. I'm his ideological adviser."

"Didn't I read in the papers that he was seriously ill?"

"Newspapers always exaggerate. The State Department may have had something to do with that story. The doctors have already found out that it's nothing serious, but he has to stay on here a few more days for a further check-up."

The little drawing room in the hotel where the Professor led me was very quiet. There was only one guest, seated in a corner, sipping a glass of milk and leafing through an illustrated weekly. He paid no attention to us; in fact, his back was turned.

"The purpose of our trip to Europe is quickly explained," the Professor went on to say. "Back home they're beginning to feel the need for reorganizing public life on authoritarian lines. Democracy has run its course, that's clear. Not to mention those plagues, freedom of the press and freedom of thought. The way I—and all who accept the principles of pantautology—look at it, the State is the State and cannot *not* be the State. Unfortunately, the liberating movement which was supposed to end up with a big March on Washington to drive the Bolshie-Jew-Negro fifth column from the White House has slowed down a little lately. So I thought up this trip to Europe, and my friend liked the idea. Your fortunate continent has enjoyed dictatorships since ancient times, and it still has some flourishing examples. Let's go in person and take a look, we decided, see for ourselves what these famous dictatorships they always talk about are really like, what sort of men these dictators are, how they got hold of power, and above all, what we can learn from their experiences. And of course we went for inspiration to the hallowed spots where the great men of the past had their tryst with destiny. For example, we stopped off at the Rubicon, where Caesar and his loyal legionaries began their march on Rome."

"The Rubicon?" A sarcastic voice interrupted him. It was the stranger sitting not far from us with his glass of milk and illustrated paper. "A muddy little brook . . . A long ride in a broken-down taxi through dusty fields, and all we got to eat at the end of it was some rotten fish in a tavern plagued with flies. That meal was largely responsible for the illness that has me stuck here now in this dreary country."

"Mr. Double You?" I exclaimed, unable to conceal my surprise.

He didn't condescend to answer, but Professor Pickup gave me a glance that removed all doubt. If the stranger himself had not so unexpectedly revealed his identity, I'd have gone on thinking him an ordinary tourist. But once I knew, it was easy for me to discern something unusual in his appearance. His face, because of a deep scar along the left cheek, was somewhat asymmetrical. His eyes were hollow and tired, with the look of the insomniac. And his lips were curved by a long habit of insolence and mockery.

"We couldn't have skipped the Rubicon, my friend," the Professor tried to explain.

"I'd like to see that Caesar of yours try to ford the Mississippi with his legionaries," Mr. Double You snickered.

"In Paris, as you can imagine, we meditated at length before Napoleon's tomb in the Invalides," the Professor went on. "In Munich, a stormtrooper kindly took us to all the beer halls which were in any way connected with the origins of National Socialism. There were quite a number of them."

"So we were, you might say, at the very fountainhead of Nazism, a fountain of beer," his friend added, giving free rein to his ill temper. "We must have been in at least thirty beer halls. Finally we couldn't stand up any longer and they put us in a cab to go back to the hotel, well soaked in Aryan spirits."

"In Milan," continued the Professor, "we visited the Square of the Holy Sepulcher, well-known as the cradle of Fascism."

"Cradle in a sepulcher—it's like the title of a horror story," his friend remarked.

Unperturbed, the Professor went on with his report. "On this trip we've made the acquaintance of a hundred and forty-seven university professors and a total of three hundred and forty-six writers, army people and ex-convicts (here's the list, you can check it for yourself). We visited the offices of two hundred and forty newspapers. We ate our way through ninety-two banquets. (Please just take a look at the list.) We're carrying back to America with us twelve crates of books on the history of ancient and modern dictatorships and another crate of relics of civil wars—all authentic and very rare."

He hesitated for a moment, then added in an undertone: "Since you're Italian, I must tell you in confidence that a Genoese collector sold us, among other things, the famous egg of Columbus."

"In a sense, you might say, it's the symbol of pantautology," I exclaimed with ill-concealed admiration.

"Very acute remark that, let me congratulate you. If our *coup d'état* is a success, this egg will finally receive the honor it deserves."

"You'll display it in the Capitol?"

"There or elsewhere, at last it will have its proper shrine."

"Won't it rot?"

"The Genoa dealer guaranteed that, thanks to a special process, at some time in the past it was fortunately petrified. What a marvelous object! Every time I think about it, I'm overcome with emotion. I don't believe there's anything in the world that can equal it in the multiplicity and intensity of its meanings. Don't you agree? An egg is already, in itself, a symbol of life; but this is an egg that never rots, hence a symbol of the eternity of life, and it's the egg of Columbus, therefore a symbol of the origins of our civilization. I believe I'm not exaggerating when I say that finding Columbus's egg is the most valuable result of our trip. But what fabulous treasures are still hidden in your country! An antiquary in Syracuse offered to sell us the terrible sword of Damocles."

"I hope that Mr. Double You didn't allow that chance to slip through his fingers. . . ."

"The price at first was very high, beyond our reach in fact. Later, the merchant lowered it considerably, but the merchandise didn't appeal to Mr. Double You."

"Is he superstitious?"

"Yes, naturally, like all men of destiny. But even without the sword of Damocles he has trouble sleeping."

Mr. Double You threw his magazine aside and turned towards me.

"What decided me to start on this tiresome trip," he said, "was my curiosity to come and find out if a technique of dictatorship really existed. To tell you the truth, I haven't learned a thing from the journey. The people we met treated us like primitive barbarians and speechified at us as if we were at an official banquet. I've glanced at the books they gave us—all naïve propaganda."

"Have you forgotten," I asked, "that the best way to learn the truth is from one's opponents? If you want to find out something interesting about capitalism, read what the socialists have written; read the Protestants on Catholicism, or anarchist revelations about the police. And vice versa."

At this point Mr. Double You made a proposal which took me by surprise.

"I'll put you to the test," he said. "Since the doctors want me to stay here another few days, would you like to give me some lessons on the subject I'm interested in?"

"I wouldn't be one bit jealous," the Professor assured me with his greenish smile.

"Naturally," Mr. Double You went on, "we wouldn't expect you to give us your time for nothing."

"I can't," I said. "I'm afraid I'm too busy. But," I added, "there's someone I could recommend instead."

"Who is he? What party does he belong to?"

"He's an Italian political exile, a man of unusual objectivity," I tried to explain. "He exercises his critical faculty on his friends as well as on his enemies."

"Has he published anything? What's his name?" the Professor inquired.

"I'm not at liberty to reveal his name," I said, "for a very simple reason. He doesn't have a proper residence permit here. He's already been expelled from various so-called democratic countries, and now he's used to living here incognito—like yourself, Mr. Double You, when you travel abroad. Only for different reasons, of course. His friends know him by the name of Thomas, and as he has a horror of euphemisms and a habit of calling things by their right name, some people have nicknamed him Thomas the Cynic. They thought this nickname would offend and discredit him, but Thomas, on the contrary, is delighted with it. Since the word "cynic" is derived from the Greek *kyon*, which means dog, Thomas feels that it gives the most accurate description of his life as a stray. And going back to the famous sect of the Cynics, founded by the Greek Antisthenes after the death of Socrates,

Thomas discovered a far less confused and ambiguous definition for his personal political credo than the banal term of "antifascism." As you know, four hundred years before the birth of Christ, the Cynics were what the right-thinking press today would call "godless" or "unpatriotic." Following Socrates's teaching, they set the practice of virtue above the formal worship of the gods, and they called no man a foreigner. But here's another fact about my friend which may arouse your curiosity: it seems that he has recently been writing a manual on "The Art of Deceiving Your Neighbor."

"That sounds like vulgar cynicism to me and not at all Socratic," the Professor remarked.

"He is rightly convinced," I replied, "that it is the deceived, not the deceivers, who will profit from his manual."

"Well," Mr. Double You concluded, "maybe he could help me while away the time here. Do you think he'll agree to do it?"

"Perhaps," I said. "Since your situation is undoubtedly bizarre, it will attract him. And he loves to argue and be contradicted. For the same reason, he prefers reading the books and newspapers of his enemies rather than those of his friends. When he has no one else to dispute with, he's even been seen arguing with himself."

2

Concerning the traditions of the political art and their defects in the age of mass civilization.

THOMAS THE CYNIC

Gentlemen, after searching the whole hotel for you, I finally—and naturally—find you in the bar. Please don't bother to stand, and I absolve you of any need for introductions. One doesn't have to be a clairvoyant to see, at one glance, which of you is the illustrious Professor Pickup and which is Mr. Double You.

MR. DOUBLE YOU

I thank you for the compliment. Come sit down with us. That hat? Oh, sit on it. It only belongs to our Professor here. What can I offer you to drink?

THOMAS THE CYNIC

A glass of wine.

PROFESSOR PICKUP

Allow us to order something more nourishing for you as well. We've all known hunger at one time or another, you know.

MR. DOUBLE YOU

I gather, Mr. Cynic, that even in this democratic country you have troubles with the police? Your life can't be any too easy.

THOMAS THE CYNIC

The conscious acceptance of troubles has always distinguished human existence from that of domestic animals—hens, sheep, official journalists, parrots and the like.

PROFESSOR PICKUP

So you're a political refugee. Or, in other words, a defeated man. Since you couldn't succeed in your own country, how can you have the nerve to pontificate about political affairs?

THOMAS THE CYNIC

You are misinformed about my past. I never fought for power, only for understanding. And since you appear to consider the state of exile incompatible with the study of political science, I must remind you, Professor, that political science has been to a great extent the creation of exiles.

PROFESSOR PICKUP

Aren't you oversimplifying history a bit?

THOMAS THE CYNIC

Not in the least. Machiavelli (we must begin with him, after all) was driven out of Florence in 1512 after the return of the Medici. The following year he was implicated in the conspiracy of Pietro Paolo Boscoli and imprisoned for three months. On leaving prison he took refuge at San Casciano and only then, far removed from active politics, after his various defeats and disillusionments, did he begin to write *The Prince*. Some decades later Jean Bodin, the French thinker who introduced the concept of sovereignty into the history of political thought, had no better luck as a practical politician. While in the service of the Duc d'Alençon he became compromised through association with the *politiques*, a sect which opposed the wars of religion. This won him the enmity of Henri III and, defeated and mortified, Bodin retired into solitude to write his treatise *De la République*.

Montesquieu, two centuries later, led a much more tranquil life. He was, in fact, a member of the Académie Française, and president of the Parliament of Bordeaux; but he wrote *L'Esprit des Lois*, his work on the division of powers, in the peace and quiet of La Brède, where he retired after a trip to England during which he learned what political liberty meant in practice.

And when it comes to the moderns, allow me to remind you of such exiles as Marx, Mazzini, Lenin, Trotsky, and Masaryk. The first of these, especially, despite his unworthy followers. In our own time, Marx—with different means and different intentions—fulfilled the same function as Machiavelli in the 1500's: he tried to clarify the real workings of the capitalistic society of his time, freeing it from the veils of German idealistic philosophy and of French humanitarianism. For this reason, he has rightly been called the Machiavelli of the proletariat.

MR. DOUBLE YOU

Now I can already see how I'll turn Professor Pickup into a great political thinker. If I take over the government, my first official act will be to send him into exile.

PROFESSOR PICKUP

You'll have to excuse him, Mr. Cynic. The tiring trip and European cooking have been very hard on his nerves.

MR. DOUBLE YOU

It wasn't so much the traveling that upset my nervous system. It was this stupid notion that by visiting countries where dictatorship has already operated, we could find some science or art of the thing that we could use later on back home.

THOMAS THE CYNIC

You're not entirely wrong, in my opinion.

PROFESSOR PICKUP

If the two of you want to fly in the face of logic, go ahead; but you're denying the evidence of history.

THOMAS THE CYNIC

Surely you'll admit that the evidence can be interpreted in various ways.

PROFESSOR PICKUP

Then why did you bring up Machiavelli just now?

THOMAS THE CYNIC

I don't believe that reading Machiavelli ever put a single prince on a throne. As to the difference between theory and practice, there's an amusing episode which happened to Machiavelli himself. When he was in Milan once as the guest of the famous *condottiere* Giovanni delle Bande Nere, his host asked him to demonstrate in the square the new military formations which Machiavelli had described in a recent treatise. For this purpose, the general placed an entire corps of infantry at his guest's disposal. Machiavelli spent two hours trying to arrange the three thousand infantrymen according to the scheme he had so clearly described in his book, but he failed. When the onlookers began to feel that they had waited long enough, what with the sun blazing down and its being well past dinnertime, Giovanni delle Bande Nere said: "Well, now I'll get you all out of this, and we can go and eat." Then, telling Machiavelli to withdraw, and with some help from the drummers, the *condottiere* swiftly assembled the troops in a variety of formations, to the admiration of all present.

PROFESSOR PICKUP

The story may not be true, but it's a good one, all the same. If you don't mind my saying so, however, this anti-intellectual mania of you European radical intellectuals is one of the causes—and not the least important one—of your political sterility. You keep crossing rivers, but you always burn your bridges after you.

MR. DOUBLE YOU

I'm neither an intellectual nor a radical nor a European, and I feel that the American Revolution was a wonderful thing precisely because, unlike the French one, it wasn't heralded by a pack of jurists, economists, philosophers, and other windbags; it wasn't trying to revive the Roman or the Athenian republic; it was just the revolution of the people living in America.

PROFESSOR PICKUP

In 1776 Benjamin Franklin was sent to France as a diplomat and as an intellectual. Do you mean to tell me he didn't learn anything there?

MR. DOUBLE YOU

I don't know. That problem isn't among the causes of my insomnia.

PROFESSOR PICKUP

For a scholar, though, it might be; and his answer would have some significance even for you, the empiricist. The true, the prime cause, of the decadence of political life today is that it's overrun with presumptuous amateurs. Anybody who has failed in some other profession thinks he can make a go of politics. Take any conversation: people who wouldn't dare discuss algebra or chemistry without having studied them will argue for hours about politics, which, of course, they have never studied either. In the old days, things were different: initiation into the art of politics was a long, hard process, and the aspirants were winnowed severely. Tacitus in his *Annals*, discussing the politics of Tiberius, spoke of *arcani imperii*, the secrets of power. Wasn't this the source of the stability of certain monarchies? Politics has its secrets, or mysteries, like any other art, mysteries into which one can be initiated only by adepts. In the days, between the fifteenth and seventeenth centuries, when men still had time to meditate and hadn't been stupefied by the daily press, in Europe there was a whole literature on the *arcana reipublicae*, the mysteries of government, known only to those who were to assist princes in the art of ruling. Even then, no doubt there was one face of government which had nothing secret about it, which even the masses could contemplate and admire from the outside. But the *arcana* maintain that this aspect is simply "simulacra," a fictitious construction, a façade behind which politics performed its mysterious rites.

MR. DOUBLE YOU

Other times, other tunes, as they say in your country.

THOMAS THE CYNIC

If you mean that politics has had its secrets in every age, then I agree with you absolutely. The literature just mentioned by our distinguished Professor, which dealt with politics as if it were an occult science, flourished in the age of absolutism when the frequent conflicts between civil and religious authorities and the decline of theology made it no longer useful or convenient to continue insisting on the divine right of kings. On the other hand, since divine investiture couldn't be replaced by popular investiture, in order not to crash against Scylla after avoiding Charybdis, authority was led to shroud itself in mystery. Gustav Freytag, a late nineteenth-century German writer, has left us a curious satire of the situation that Professor Pickup has just described. He reproduces a once-popular manual on the art of governing, the *Ratio Status* of 1666, and makes an amusing parody of it. The young man who is considered suited to the position of adviser to the prince is led into the hidden apartments where the *Arcana Status* are jealously kept, the secrets which are a part of his new position: the state uniforms, the state masks, the state eyeglasses, wool for pulling over eyes, etc. There are special state cloaks, which give the proper authority and solemnity to those who wear them; these are called *salus populi, bonum publicum, conservatio religionis,* according to whether they are

being used to squeeze new taxes from the subjects or
to send them into exile or to seize the property of the
opposition under the always-useful pretext that they
are spreading heretical doctrines. One of these cloaks
is almost threadbare from daily use; it is called *in-
tentio*, good intentions, and can be used to justify
anything. With the state eyeglasses, any illusion can
be created. They allow one to see what doesn't exist,
or not to see what does; they enlarge unimportant
matters and diminish grave events. But the same results are achieved now with far simpler staging. The
plebeian myth of the sovereignty of the people has
stripped authority of these trappings.

PROFESSOR PICKUP

Parody is the most fatuous of literary forms.
For that matter, to my knowledge, the King and
Queen of England, our President, and the President
of the Soviet Union are not in the habit of appearing
at great public ceremonies in bathing suits.

THOMAS THE CYNIC

It would be childish to confuse truth with nudism.

MR. DOUBLE YOU

What is truth? You're right, Mr. Cynic, a crowd
of bathers doesn't represent truth any better than a
masked ball. But the two things are different—you
can't deny that.

THOMAS THE CYNIC

Pontius Pilate also asked what truth was, in vain,
even though he had it before his eyes. But he was a
Roman governor, and truth isn't a state activity. It's

not just a question of plumes or uniforms. With to-day's mass civilization it isn't absurd to suggest that in some rich, advanced and neutral country, power might one day be seized, for example, by a coalition of athletic clubs. In that case, we might have a sports-man in shorts or a beauty queen in a bathing suit at the helm of the state. But even then, public affairs would not become crystal clear. The organization of sports is now as much of an oligarchy as any party executive, and horse races, boxing matches, and beauty contests also have their official secrets. But merely from a practical point of view, I would like to insist on the fact that these mysteries are different from those of a conclave of the Catholic Church or of the Soviet Communist Party's Politburo.

PROFESSOR PICKUP

They're not all that different. The way I look at it, times change, but men don't. Machiavelli was correct in writing about the immutability of human nature throughout the changing centuries: "The world has always been inhabited by the same kind of men who have always had the same passions." And it's no coincidence that Mussolini tells how, when he was a boy, his father used to read *The Prince* to him every Saturday evening.

THOMAS THE CYNIC

From what we know of Mussolini's father, I'd rule out the possibility that he was in a fit state to do any reading on Saturday nights. It was only his mania for pomp—like his using mediaeval uniforms or riding horses—that made Mussolini invent that legend. Luckily for him, all his life he had read—and still reads—nothing but newspapers. But, talented news-paperman that he is, he has a facility for talking and writing arrogantly on things he knows nothing about. As a proof of his cocksureness in the realm of intelligence, there is a revealing detail mentioned in Signora Sarfatti's official biography. After reading Nietzsche's *Thus Spake Zarathustra,* the first more or less philosophical book he had ever run into (cheap editions of it were widely read by anarchist workers in pre-war Italy), Mussolini decided to write a universal history of philosophy. He believed he already knew enough about the subject.

PROFESSOR PICKUP

That's a detail I hadn't heard, and I must honestly say I can't pronounce on it. But you will recall, I hope, what Hitler confesses in *Mein Kampf.* "World history," he says, "has always provided me with an inexhaustible fund of suggestions for political action in the present."

THOMAS THE CYNIC

Do you know the kind of world history he means? According to his biographers, young Adolf's favorite reading was two bound volumes of an illustrated weekly about the Franco-Prussian war of 1870-71. Even later, as *Mein Kampf* amply proves, his knowledge of famous generals and their battles continued to be derived from popular magazines.

PROFESSOR PICKUP

And in spite of that, Mussolini and Hitler were able to seize power in two of the most civilized countries in the world? If what you say is true, Mr. Cynic, I find their victory incomprehensible.

THOMAS THE CYNIC

This simply means that the explanation of their success mustn't be sought—as you claim it should—in any superior knowledge on their part of the so-called laws of history or politics. Among their political opponents there were surely men who knew far more than either of them did.

PROFESSOR PICKUP

And yet, if I'm not mistaken, the Fascist and Nazi victories took the majority of democratic or liberal spokesmen by surprise.

THOMAS THE CYNIC

Yes, but you know why? Their political and social theory had stopped at 1914. Consequently, for them, the greatest danger to civil liberties still lay with the traditional conservative forces. I repeat, however, that it wasn't a question of Mussolini and Hitler being more up to date intellectually; it was simply that they were men of the war generation, new men, men of instinct, and they were already up to their necks in the new social reality.

PROFESSOR PICKUP

When we were in Rome we met a Fascist writer whose pen name is a play on Napoleon's surname. In a conversation with us, he maintained that the conquest and defense of the state isn't a question of politics but of technology, and that the circumstances favoring a *coup d'état* aren't necessarily political or social and don't depend on the general situation of the country. According to him, the technical centralization of modern life permits the maximum spatial limitation of the area of the *coup*. He has developed this concept in a book which he gave us, called *The Technique of the Coup d'État*. It seems that the Italian authorities have banned this book to keep opponents of the regime from making use of it.

THOMAS THE CYNIC

Trotsky, who is mentioned as a model in that book and praised above Lenin, has written a masterful demolition of it; but the work didn't deserve such an honor. The tendency to consider politics as a mere technique is an intellectual leftover from the Renaissance. It's related to the similar tendency of the artists of that period to consider their works as technical rather than aesthetic problems. Today, we are aware that if the paintings of the Renaissance masters still move us, this happens despite their technique and not because of it; and as for the vicissitudes of Renaissance Florence, it would take some doing to explain them away now as a mere mechanical game. What's equally out of date, of course, is the Romantic concept of the revolutionary *coup d'état* which the Frenchman Blanqui evolved in the last century. And incidentally, although the trend of political life almost everywhere now has moved away from the old system of small, well-differentiated parties of opinion toward that of amorphous mass parties, this hasn't made the game of politics one bit simpler. On the contrary. No politician can afford to be ignorant about economic and social questions any longer. It's only in the realm of fantasy that the technical centralization of modern life makes you think it would be easy to overthrow a government if you could seize and occupy two or three buildings in the Capital. Not even the most backward populace allows itself to be boarded like a ship. In fact, in a regime having several parties and newspapers of several tendencies, this very mass civilization makes it more difficult to bring off a *coup d'état*. The operation has to be political even before it can be technical. But you need go no farther than the book itself for proof that Signor Malaparte's theory is frivolous. Since at the very moment when he was engaged in writing it, his main thesis was being disproved by the difficult struggle in which the Nazi movement had been engaged for years, Malaparte concluded that Herr Hitler would never achieve power.

MR. DOUBLE YOU

If the old art of politics is out of date, and the new one hasn't yet reached the bookshops, what course would you suggest for a well-intentioned man who aspires to the dictatorship of his country?

THOMAS THE CYNIC

He should proceed like a man in a city that has been devastated by an earthquake: with one eye on the map and the other looking around him. In every new or transitory situation, instinct is worth more than knowledge, for all practical purposes. But instinct is a quality that can't be taught. Mussolini himself said this very effectively, almost in pantautological terms: "The public man is born public. It's a stigma that's with him from birth. One is born a public man, just as one is born intelligent or simple-minded. There is no apprenticeship that can make a public figure out of a man whose tendency is towards domestic life."

MR. DOUBLE YOU

Democracy has helped many a hen to fly.

THOMAS THE CYNIC

Napoleon Bonaparte was almost totally ignorant of the history of Europe, which is why it was easier for him to turn it inside out. He became a great strategist and even a great legislator, thanks, as Metternich wrote, "to his instinct alone." But to return to our own times, I advise you to read the admirable portrait of Stalin drawn by Boris Souvarine. You'll be amazed by the disproportion, in Lenin's successor, between intelligence and the will to succeed, between his knowledge and his cunning. "Patient, meticulous, with as few illusions as words, and strong, above all, in his contempt for the individual, in his lack of principles and scruples. He is a product of circumstances," Souvarine says. "He owes his political fortune to his opponents. He would never have succeeded in imposing himself without a certain sixth sense, a natural capacity for intrigue, and an effective blend of energy and cold-bloodedness. Adept at postponing unpleasant decisions, at dividing his enemies and avoiding obstacles, he stops at nothing when he sees the chance to hurry on, to strike, and to crush." But perhaps we can sum it up by saying that all the most successful politicians have been opportunists of genius.

PROFESSOR PICKUP

If it's instinct rather than knowledge that's the decisive requisite in practical politics, how do you explain the fact that in Berlin and Rome they've set up political schools for training new leaders?

THOMAS THE CYNIC

In spite of their pompous name, they're just seminaries for the training of bureaucrats. They are meant to prepare obedient, devoted party workers. They are meant not to create new Hitlers and Mussolinis, but to make sure there will be no new ones.

MR. DOUBLE YOU

That's enough for today. May I say something that concerns you both? The two of you quote too much. Couldn't you manage without quotations?

PROFESSOR PICKUP

Then the conversation would become personal, whereas the subject isn't.

THOMAS THE CYNIC

And if you want to become a dictator, you'll have to get used to quotations. A dictatorship is a regime in which people quote instead of thinking. They all quote a single book that serves as a sacred text. We at least have the advantage of being able to quote various authors.

MR. DOUBLE YOU

Perhaps these quotations get on my nerves because they remind me of school.

THOMAS THE CYNIC

Well, the word dictatorship comes from dictation, after all, and that too is a scholastic exercise. But dictatorship is more disagreeable, since it has only one classroom and spelling mistakes are punished by the police.

3.

Concerning certain conditions which favor totalitarian tendencies in our time.

PROFESSOR PICKUP

May I have the privilege of opening today's conversation? Thank you. To begin with, I'd like to demonstrate the usefulness of quotation, which Mr. Cynic so rightly defended at the end of our meeting yesterday. I would like to remind you of what Aristotle wrote in the fifth book of his *Politics* about the causes of the fall of the Hellenic democracies. Democracies, Aristotle says, are inherently prone to revolutions rising out of the excesses of the demagogues. Since every demagogue tries to exploit the rich under a cloak of flattery, the rich are often driven to unite in self-defense; on other occasions the demagogues openly act as rabble-rousers against the rich.

The experience of the Greeks is important because history has seen only one crop of dictatorships that can be compared, in size, to today's, and that was during the seventh and sixth centuries B.C. in the Hellenic world. The majority of the Greek city-states were ravaged by furious civil struggles, in which an aristocratic and a democratic party fought each other for power. What usually happened was that a member of one of the old aristocratic families placed himself at the head of the people and, once he had seized power, wielded it tyrannically, exiling the rival aristocratic families, confiscating their property and distributing it among his own followers. Historians tell us, too, that the aspiring dictator's party consisted of mercenaries, less devoted to the interests of

the city than to those of their captain and his family,
and of plebeian malcontents filled with hatred of the
aristocracy that exploited them. The use of soldiers
in factional quarrels became possible at that period,
thanks to a new army system according to which anyone was a soldier who possessed weapons of his own.
In this way many became soldiers and risked their
lives for their city, even though they had no voice in
the city's councils. The captain who could gain a
personal ascendancy over the new recruits had an easy
opportunity to make use of them for seizing power.
So the chronicles tell us how—when Athens was divided between the two rival factions of the Pedieis
and the Parali—rich landlords and small holders re-
spectively—the noble Peisistratus, son of Hippocrates,
founded a third faction, in which he enrolled the most
turbulent elements of the plebeian population, well-
known to him and under his influence since the time
of their military service with him. Among them
Peisistratus chose fifty who were particularly strong
and daring, and armed them with staves (*koruneforoi*).
Then, with their help, he occupied the Acropolis and
set himself up as dictator of Athens. And one last
point: for the Greeks the word "tyrant" didn't have
the pejorative meaning that it later acquired. The
tyrant was often a democrat.

THOMAS THE CYNIC
    That can happen in our own time, too.

MR. DOUBLE YOU
    Let's come down to our own time, then. There's
a French poet we had to visit because he's so famous.
Paul Valéry is his name. He admitted, while talking

to us, that the idea of dictatorship is contagious now-adays, the way the idea of freedom was in the last century. What's the cause of this epidemic? Are we to consider it a world-wide and lasting phenomenon? I ask myself this because, according to a popular saying which a mediocre American novelist has made into a kind of slogan, Fascism can't happen in our country.

PROFESSOR PICKUP

Well, if we're on the subject of the instability of regimes, I suppose Machiavelli's classic argument is still the last word. According to him, no form is stable, since virtue generates calm; calm, idleness; idleness, anarchy; anarchy, ruin. And, similarly, from ruin there arises, by reaction, a longing for order; from order comes virtue; and from virtue, glory and good fortune. The way Machiavelli describes it, you'd think he was talking about a process of nature, but it's easy to see that all these terms—virtue, calm, idleness, anarchy, ruin, glory—really refer to moral concepts.

THOMAS THE CYNIC

Why did Germany have Bismarck at one stage and Hitler now? Do you think a regime such as Hitler's would have been conceivable even a little while ago—say in 1910?

MR. DOUBLE YOU

Ah, that's the question.

PROFESSOR PICKUP

Mr. Cynic is right, you can't fly in the face of time. Spengler answers your question with his theory of the rise and decline of civilizations, which com-pletes Machiavelli's thought and brings it up to date. Decadence afflicts empires and republics as old age afflicts man. There's no escaping it. To what extent is America involved today in the decline of the West? I find certain points of his brilliant diagnosis seem more relevant to our country than to Europe, others perhaps less. At the very worst, the choice will be our own, and here too I agree with Spengler. Our duty, he says, is to stand fast at our post, even without hope. To stand fast like that Roman soldier whose bones were found outside a gate at Pompeii, where he died because when Vesuvius erupted somebody forgot to release him from his duty.

MR. DOUBLE YOU

Who told Spengler that soldier was there on guard duty and not just waiting for a girl who was standing him up?

PROFESSOR PICKUP

Obviously everyone has the imagination he de-serves.

THOMAS THE CYNIC

Spengler has the imagination of a decadent lit-terateur. Up to a few years ago his German followers used to delight in playing Cassandra and predicting the inevitable end of Europe. (A fine consolation for the people whose savings had vanished with inflation: we're ruined, all right, but ha ha, the others will soon get what they deserve too). Now, ever since the victory of Hitler's National Socialism, they've been singing joyous hymns to the eternal youth of the

German people and the evergreen Nordic forest. The very ones who had already donned the tunic of the Roman soldier and were scanning the horizon for signs of the volcano erupting are now selling beer and frankfurters on outings of the *Kraft durch Freude* organization.

MR. DOUBLE YOU

This fantasy of nations being born and growing up and growing old seems a lot of hot air to me, too. Can't disorder, instability and violent change happen just as easily to a young nation? But we've had enough digressions about terms and historical laws and primal causes. Mr. Cynic, let's get down to facts.

THOMAS THE CYNIC

We can begin, if you both agree, with certain present aspects of the crisis of democratic institutions, which can be found in all countries.

MR. DOUBLE YOU

Could you do me a favor and leave out the word "crisis"? It has too many meanings; it really doesn't mean anything specific nowadays.

THOMAS THE CYNIC

If the word annoys you, I'll try to avoid it. Now then, the first point to which I would like to draw your attention is the general tendency toward *étatisme*, by which democracy, while trying to achieve its nature, devours itself. This is a fate which, I believe, it is hard for democracy to escape. A democracy is in duty bound to assist the masses, and even capitalists when they are in trouble; and this it can do only by overloading the old liberal institutions with an ever greater number of tasks. The result everywhere is an increase in areas of power, of a kind and a quantity that no political democracy can possibly control. Thus the so-called sovereignty of the people is more than ever reduced to a fiction. The State budget reaches monstrous proportions, which not even specialists can make head or tail of. Real sovereignty passes into the hands of the bureaucracy, which by definition is anonymous and irresponsible, while the legislative bodies begin to look like gatherings of old windbags squabbling over trifles. As the legislative function declines, it is inevitable that the average moral standard of the legislator will also decline. Members of Parliament no longer care about anything except getting re-elected. In order to repay the favors of the pressure groups on whose support their re-election depends, they need the good will of the administration. The organs of local government, the so-called intermediary powers, all traditional and spontaneous forms of social existence die out. Or, if they survive, they are rendered meaningless.

Now the hegemony of a centralized administration is the premise of every dictatorship; indeed, it already *is* dictatorship. And while I don't mean to imply that this is necessarily a process of cause-and-effect; at the same time, we see everywhere a growing estrangement from traditional beliefs. The great myths that nourished the faith of our forefathers seem to be generally outworn, at least insofar as they are reflected in public life. Oh yes, the temples survive, the liturgies, the emblems, the hymns, but where is the enthusiasm? Does anyone delude himself any more that a belief in the same God can improve relations among peoples,

or that the Christian ethic is applicable in social relationships?

The internationalism of the labor movement, on
the other hand, although younger, has fared no better.
Among the moderate members, it has ended up in
various forms of social patriotism, and with the extremists, in subjugation to Soviet imperialism. Socialism has been nationalized almost everywhere, like the
railways and the postal system. And as far as I know,
toastmasters at banquets no longer raise their glasses
to the Gradual, Inevitable Progress of Humanity and
the humanistic role of the sciences. Nobody believes
in all that any more. Every thinking person now
knows for certain that the alternative—decline and
destruction—is also possible. This is the spiritual
plight of the elite in almost every civilized country
today. As a result, these elites have nothing valid with
which to oppose the encroachment of mass civilization, nothing which would appeal even to that limited
part of the public which is open to the higher forms
of culture. The encroachment of mass civilization can
be seen in the enormous spread of the so-called mass
media, with the result that people's attitude and out-
look conform increasingly to a single pattern and
they become incapable of using their brains.

MR. DOUBLE YOU

I recognize the picture. Everything you have
mentioned already exists in our country, more or less.
But we don't have a dictatorship yet.

THOMAS THE CYNIC

In the same way, a certain rate of cholesterol in
the blood makes heart disease possible but not in-

evitable. Given the conditions I have described, for a political collapse to take place the state of general insecurity must be so acute that people are desperate and dictatorship is invoked even by many of its opponents.

MR. DOUBLE YOU

We'll discuss that another day.

4.

Outline of a coup d'état *after an abortive revolution.*

MR. DOUBLE YOU

I can't understand why Fascism appeared first in a country like Italy, where the conditions of mass civilization—which you described in our last conversation—are certainly less developed than in America.

THOMAS THE CYNIC

People make that same objection to sociological explanations of the Russian Revolution. I feel that Trotsky's answer is valid for all cases of this kind. When a chain is tested, he says, it always breaks at its relatively weakest link. You must remember our situation at the end of the Great War. The war had disrupted the old relationships among countries and among the different classes of the population. The countries without economic reserves, the defeated countries, the structurally weak countries like Italy, the countries created by the peace treaty—all these had an extremely stormy existence. What happened afterward was certainly not inevitable; there are always several possible solutions for every crisis, the only Utopian solution being, in such cases, the *status quo.* As it happened, many democrats and liberals cherished this dream of a conservative Utopia, unable to discern, in the anarchy surrounding them, anything beyond its psychological aspects, the so-called "war psychosis," and hoping that the situation would slowly calm down and they could go back to the

1914 way of life. But society was no longer what it had been then.

MR. DOUBLE YOU

When you were telling us the conditions that favor a *coup d'état*, you didn't mention the necessity of saving society from the threat of a communist revolution. Did you leave that out on purpose? As you can imagine, this is a very important point for me. I'd be a fool if I sat around waiting for that kind of danger to arise in the United States.

THOMAS THE CYNIC

Let me reassure you: I don't find the condition you specify at all indispensable for the success of a *coup d'état*.

MR. DOUBLE YOU

But both Mussolini and Hitler claim to have saved their countries from an imminent communist revolution.

THOMAS THE CYNIC

After you've won, nobody can prevent you from inventing the same legend. It's true that in Italy at the end of 1922, as in Germany in the spring of 1933, the political chaos could have ended in various ways, but a communist seizure of power was not among them.

PROFESSOR PICKUP

If you don't mind my saying so, Mr. Cynic, I have the feeling that you're pretty cynical in deciding what came first and what came afterward. How can

you deny that in the two countries in question the
workers were the first to attack and were still in
fighting trim? For that matter, the Marxists never
made any secret of it. We can skip the old 1848
Manifesto, but in the years just before the Great War,
and for some years after it, the same challenge was
repeated in every possible key. According to the
Marxists, humanity was at that time "suffering" in
peace and prosperity, and in his *Reflections on Violence* Georges Sorel wondered how to rekindle the
dying embers of revolutionary ardor in the bourgeoisie.
This was precisely the task of proletarian violence—
to make every bourgeois conscious of the class to
which he belonged. How worried Sorel was, seeing
the industrialists give in to the claims of social reform and concern themselves with health and accident
insurance, sporting clubs and sanitary housing for
their workers. To see the bourgeoisie trying to limit
its own strength filled poor Sorel with sadness. Fortunately proletarian violence sometimes forced the bourgeois to resume their function as producers, and
restored the class distinctions which were tending to
disappear. Capitalist society, in Sorel's opinion, would
achieve its "historical perfection" in proportion to the
extent to which proletariat and capital remained irreconcilable and fought each other in a warlike
spirit. After decades of anticipation the battle, heralded
by a great deal of shouting, has finally taken place. To
use Sorel's words, society has achieved its historical
perfection in various ways. The Marxists have won
in Russia, almost by surprise and with the help of a
number of extraordinary circumstances. They have
been beaten and rendered helpless in the Balkans, in
the Baltic countries, in Italy, Germany and South

America. In other countries the struggle is only beginning, and we needn't think that the Marxists are
standing by as idle spectators. But when the Marxists
get beaten in the battles that they've started themselves, I don't understand why they complain so much
and hurl accusations of violence at the other side.

THOMAS THE CYNIC

In the first place, my dear Professor, you are
mistaken if you take Sorel as a representative of the
labor movement. In Italy, where his influence was
undoubtedly more widespread and more active than
in his native France, his only followers were a few
intellectuals, who in 1914 were among the leaders of
the campaign to bring Italy into the war, and in 1919
were among the founders of the first *Fasci*. But you
cannot rightly understand Sorel's ideas about violence
if you divorce them from his fundamental belief,
namely that it is useless to cloak the real antagonisms
of society with hypocritical draperies, for when that
happens the content of social existence is falsified,
moral and intellectual decadence results, and even
production itself declines. That was why Sorel was
so fiercely opposed to parliamentary socialism and its
spirit of cooperation and why he hoped for a class
struggle without intermediaries, a straight fight between workers and entrepreneurs. But to prove to
you that Sorel was in no way responsible for fascist
violence, I need only say one thing; the net result of
fascist violence was to shift the axis of the political
struggle from the objective, historical frontiers of
party and class, replacing them with a contrived national or racial unity. By different means and with
different consequences, fascist violence thus fulfilled

the function that before the war had been entrusted to social reformism, which Sorel had opposed as being reactionary and immoral. But to get back to the original question, I must insist on the falsity of the notion that socialism was defeated by fascism in both Italy and Germany. The truth is that Fascism in Italy and Nazism in Germany were both born out of the socialist defeat.

PROFESSOR PICKUP

Well, who did defeat socialism in those countries then?

THOMAS THE CYNIC

In both countries, socialism defeated itself. In the social and political anarchy that prevailed in post-war Italy and Germany from the armistice onwards, social-ism appeared to the masses as the only force capable of satisfying their aspirations and giving society a new order. But in both countries socialism was spir-itually divided into roughly two currents: a revolu-tionary current aiming—at least in words—at imme-diate expropriation of the wealthy classes and the dictatorship of the proletariat, and a reformist current aiming at a gradual peaceful improvement of the conditions of the poor. In Italy the two currents neutralized each other, so that the reformists made no attempt at reform, and the revolutionaries no attempt at revolution. In Germany the Social Democrats were partners to the crushing of the Spartacus Union and they never made any serious or vigorous attempt to introduce radical democratic reform, let alone to re-place the tottering structure of German capitalism with a socialist economy. Instead, as people said at the

time, "The Kaiser departed and the generals remained." On the other hand, a revolutionary situation
doesn't last for many years, and if the revolutionary
party fails to exploit it quickly, the disappointed
masses turn away and passively accept the opposing
party or actually put it in power. In Italy this reversal
of the situation took place after the workers occupied
the factories. The evacuation of the factories broke
the impetus of the workers and demoralized them,
showing them that the party in which they had placed
their hope was capable only of speechifying. Up to
1923 the German Socialists had a chance to intervene
decisively in reorganizing the country; but they, too,
ended by capitulating without a struggle. The German
and Italian workers consequently had to face the first
onrush of fascist violence at a time when they were
already retreating in disorder from the advanced
positions they had hastily occupied, more by surprise
than by force, in the first months after the armistice.

The new situation was immediately exploited by
most reactionary groups. They made the working
classes bear the brunt of the economic and financial
instability and countered the competition of foreign
industry by cutting wages at home. When the danger
of revolution was past, thanks to the internal flaws of
socialism, and even before fascism had come to represent a political force, the middle class encouraged
Mussolini and Hitler to transform the retreat of the
workers' organizations into a rout and to inflict
crushing defeat on the too costly policy of gradual
social reform. The nature of this struggle was more
strikingly apparent in Italy than in Germany. In Italy
its development was more rapid and the political views
of its Fascist leader were more flexible than those of

Hitler. It's beyond doubt that after its early patriotic phase, Fascism emerged and developed as a reaction against social reformism rather than against communist revolutionary socialism. The rich peasants, the shop-keepers, the small industrialists who joined Mussolini's *Fasci* in 1921 did so in order to combat the incon-venient reformist movement, which, especially for small businesses, had reduced profits to a minimum. Take the provinces of the Po valley, where in forty years of peaceful activity the reformists had created a well-knit group of farmers' unions, cooperatives, and insurance and credit organizations, controlling a large part of the economic life of the region, and in some sectors exercising an actual monopoly. There the Fascist reaction was at its bloodiest. And this is easily understood. The soapbox revolutionaries with their noisy and inconclusive rallies endangered nothing but the streetlights and occasionally the bones of some policeman. But reformism, even without any great political prospects, devoting all its energies to working patiently, methodically and legally, was threatening something far more sacred: the profits of private enterprise. Not the profits of the big banks, from which the reformists themselves needed and obtained credit, but the profits of the small private entrepreneurs. Against mere windbag revolutionaries, the bourgeoisie felt that the laws of the State were sufficient defense; but against peaceful, law-abiding reformism they needed the Fascist terrorist gangs; they needed to destroy that legality by which they no longer felt protected. Later, Fascist violence was also directed against both the revolutionary socialists and the communists, just at the moment when both had lost all hope of an immediate revolution and, to avoid being cut off from the masses, had begun defending the worker's living conditions and were fighting the battle for higher wages with a pugnacity that was upsetting the opportunist calculations of the reformist leaders, who by this time had been terrorized by the Fascist attack and were prepared to conclude a peace treaty with the Fascists. The subsequent developments and complications mustn't make us forget this initial truth: Fascism was a counter-revolution against a revolution that never took place.

MR. DOUBLE YOU

What you say sounds convincing enough. But do you really believe that exactly the same pattern of events could be repeated anywhere else?

THOMAS THE CYNIC

I don't know. In any case I'd like to summarize my ideas as follows. For a totalitarian system to be able to take over, the first condition is that there should be a paralysis of the democratic state, that is to say, an irremediable breach between the old political system on the one hand, and a radically transformed social system on the other. The second condition is that the collapse of the state should at first benefit the old opposition party and lead the masses to it as being the only party capable of establishing a new order. The third condition is that this party will prove itself inadequate for the difficult task, and in fact, by disappointing the hopes placed in it, will merely add to the already existing anarchy. When these conditions have been fulfilled, and everyone is at the end of his tether, the totalitarian party bursts upon the scene. If its leader isn't a complete imbecile, it stands a good chance of getting into power.

MR. DOUBLE YOU

Let's stop for a moment at the third phase of your outline: the failure of the traditional opposition party, which—if I follow you—may be either social-ist or conservative, or just plain democratic. I wonder if the experiences of Italy, Germany, the Balkans, and Latin America are of any relevance to other countries. We mustn't overlook one detail: Fascism so far has taken over only in places where the roots of democ-racy were rather superficial.

PROFESSOR PICKUP

Forgive me for interrupting a moment. In my opinion, the inferiority of democracy to fascism lies in the inadequacy of the democratic ideal, which postulates an absurdity: the sovereignty of the people.

THOMAS THE CYNIC

Personally I think that the greatest weakness of the democratic system today lies in the fact that it is conservative. He who stops while society moves on is trampled to death. There is a great difference be-tween the democrats of our day and their ancestors, the ones who fought on the barricades, in civil wars and wars of independence, for civil liberties and for the political and juridical equality of every citizen. This difference doesn't lie in individual talents or character. The political and juridical equality of every citizen was, at that time, a novelty and an ideal. As such it had a fascination that inflamed all men of spirit; they espoused the cause of the people and fought beside the people against the court, nobility, clergy or foreign domination. Today's democrats no longer have any ideal to work for. They are living on the income from the achievements of their ancestors.

A successful revolutionary movement enhances its protagonists and lends them the gigantic stature of the pioneers, of the Cromwells, the Robespierres, the Jeffersons, Mazzinis and Lenins. A democracy in decline, which keeps alive by dint of compromises and expedients, can only be governed by men like Facta and Bruning, Laval and Chamberlain; and the more time passes, the lower it is to be feared that the standard will fall. Of course it's possible that bourgeois democracy may still find spokesmen of great distinction, but I believe that this is more likely to occur in countries where such democracy has never existed, in feudal, semi-feudal and colonial countries which have arrived only recently at the threshold of the so-called bourgeois revolution. Think of men like Sun Yat Sen and Gandhi and compare them to our democratic prime ministers, the ones I have just mentioned. They all belong to the same historic movement, but the former are at its dawn and the latter at its sunset. The leaders of European democracy, in short, display all the characteristics of a political class that has outlived its mission.

PROFESSOR PICKUP

Goebbels says that the success of National Socialism was due in great part to the stupidity of its opponents. They had control of everything: the army, the police, the bureaucracy, the banks, the parliamentary majority, the radio, the big newspapers—and they just didn't know how to make use of it all.

THOMAS THE CYNIC

If you judge from that point of view, every change of regime seems the product of the stupidity of the old ruling class, taken by surprise. There is no lack of historians who attempt to show that if Louis XVI had done this or that, or if Tsarist circles in 1917 had taken this or that precaution, neither the French nor the Russian Revolution would have taken place. The same thing could easily be said of all the other revolutions, which—to the superficial eye—always have something incomprehensible about them. It is true that every ruling class has at its disposal, up to the very day the regime falls, all the necessary material means with which to defend itself. But it lacks the will, the ability, the courage to use them, and these are the essential attributes of men who would rule. Before being physically defeated and dispossessed, the old ruling class has already been spiritually vanquished. Shortsighted, spineless, without a head, suffering from the senile diseases of formalism and legalism, it manages to keep on its feet through sheer inertia. It continues to worship formulas and to entrench itself behind formal respect of the law and legal procedure, but these are of more help to the opposition than to the democracy itself, and by this time their effect is the opposite of what was originally intended.

PROFESSOR PICKUP

The exploitation of democratic legality in order to destroy democracy was, in fact, a process well understood by both Fascists and National Socialists. Democracy, as Hitler wrote in *Mein Kampf*, is at best a means for paralyzing the opponent. In 1935, two years after the Nazis had seized power, Goebbels boasted of having brought it off. "We always declared," he wrote, "that we would use democratic methods to gain power, and that once in power we would deny our enemies all the opportunities which we ourselves had enjoyed when in opposition." For that matter, communists in democratic countries have much the same attitude towards the law.

THOMAS THE CYNIC

The democrats are aware of this, but they are powerless to do anything about it. A ruling class in decline lives by half-measures from day to day, and keeps putting off vital issues until tomorrow. When forced to make a decision, it appoints committees and subcommittees, which complete their investigation when the situation has already changed. To be late in these cases means to lock the stable door after the horse is stolen. It also gives the illusion that one is dodging responsibility, washing one's hands to show future historians how white and pure they are. For democrats in troubled countries, the height of the art of governing seems to consist in accepting slaps so as to avoid kicks, in bearing the lesser evil, in constantly thinking up new compromises for minimizing disagreements and reconciling the irreconcilable.

The enemies of democracy take advantage of this and grow daily more insolent. They conspire in broad daylight, they store up arms, they have their followers parade in the streets in military formations, they attack—ten to one—the most hated democratic leaders. The government, "weighing its words so as not to worsen the situation," deplores the events and hopes "for the nation's good name" that they weren't premeditated, and makes fervent appeals to the citizenry that "peace may return to all hearts." The important thing, in the minds of the democratic leaders, is to avoid any words and measures likely to irritate the

seditious elements and make the situation worse. If the
police find out that certain political and military leaders have compromised themselves with the rebel organization and helped supply weapons, the government may grow bolder and, as a warning, have a few
of the lesser conspirators arrested. Never the leaders,
because that would provoke a scandal and hasten the
catastrophe. The responsible leaders of the democracy
know that they have everything to lose and nothing to
gain by exacerbating political relations. So they imagine they're gaining time by playing the ostrich game.
Thus the young Spanish republic reprieved Sanjurjo
and kept the monarchist generals at the head of the
army, even when it was common knowledge that they
were preparing a *coup d'état*. In the same way Mussolini was never held responsible for the Fascist outrages perpetrated throughout the country by armed
bands under his direction and at his orders. Officers,
even generals, were still kept on in the army after they
had joined the *Fasci*. It was the same in Germany.
"To contribute to the pacification of all hearts," the
German republic reprieved Ludendorff after von
Kapp's unsuccessful putsch in 1920, and after Hitler's
premature one in 1923, and it left unpunished the
leaders of the "Consul" terrorist organization who had
ordered the assassination of two ministers, Erzberger
and Rathenau, even though there was no doubt as to
the identity of those who were responsible.

MR. DOUBLE YOU

In Berlin we met Baron von Killinger and the
Duke of Coburg, President of the German Red Cross,
both of them leaders of the "Consul" organization
from its beginning. They told us in great detail how

the assassinations were arranged. They boast publicly about them now, and about the fact that, even under a democratic regime, they scarcely bothered to conceal their responsibility. Their courage, to tell the truth, was in proportion to the cowardice of the men who ruled the Republic.

THOMAS THE CYNIC

But there were, however, some democrats who were neither cowardly nor passive, and who paid with their lives—or with prison, deportation or exile—for the fact that they stood by their principles. But they were isolated figures no longer able to count on their traditional supporters, the middle classes, and still less on the working class, now that it had been frustrated in its revolutionary hopes.

MR. DOUBLE YOU

Don't you think that what happened in Italy and Germany has taught democrats in other countries something?

THOMAS THE CYNIC

What sort of thing? As long as the situation remains good, everyone is convinced that in his own country certain things could never happen. When the cyclone hits, the watchword is: Every man for himself. The truth is that a declining political class has all the infirmities of old age, including deafness. Necker, the finance minister of Louis XVI, sent warnings and advice to his king, but to no avail. How many warnings did Tsar Nicholas II receive? Had he been capable of understanding them, he would not have been the Tsar. A declining political class not only lacks the ability, resolve and the courage to use the means at its disposal in order to govern and to defend itself from the attacks of its enemies, but it no longer has even the intelligence to dominate the constantly changing situation or to understand what is going on. All these factors encourage totalitarian enterprises.

MR. DOUBLE YOU

Why do you so often say "totalitarian" instead of "fascist"? Is it because you don't want to offend the communists?

THOMAS THE CYNIC

Precisely. But also out of due regard for the dictatorial possibilities latent in any determined group of democrats or liberals.

MR. DOUBLE YOU

You're joking, I suppose. Apart from the fact that, after everything you've said, such a notion seems unreal to me, do you really believe that there could possibly be such a thing as a democratic totalitarianism?

THOMAS THE CYNIC

Why not? I'm thinking of a totalitarianism along Jacobin lines, openly democratic in its ideals and antidemocratic in its methods, because of the backward condition of the masses. This may be the most practicable political form for the democratic leaders of colonial peoples, when they achieve independence.

MR. DOUBLE YOU

Forgive me for asking a personal question: am I

right in thinking that your preference is for a party of this sort?

THOMAS THE CYNIC

Not any longer. Not since I realized that in due course the end is replaced by the means.

5.

*Concerning the aspiring dictator's
unrequited love for the Muses, the
insignificance of family trees, and the
inevitability of severe headaches.*

PROFESSOR PICKUP

Mr. Double You's doctor has sent for him, and he
asks you to forgive him for this unexpected inconvenience.

THOMAS THE CYNIC

It's perfectly all right. I can come back later, or
whenever he likes.

PROFESSOR PICKUP

No, please stay. Since he wasn't able to let you
know in time, today's conversation will naturally be
counted, as usual.

THOMAS THE CYNIC

In that case, allow me to invite you to the bar. We
must drink a glass of wine to his health.

PROFESSOR PICKUP

Gladly. But let's not sit too close to the orchestra.
Mr. Double You's accidental absence gives me the
chance to confide something to you. Though it's of a
personal nature, it concerns the fundamental topic of
our conversations. Yesterday you happened to mention that the personality of the aspiring dictator plays
a decisive role in the success of his undertaking? Well,
I hope you won't think I'm being disloyal, but I must

confess to you that I have grave doubts about Mr. Double You's suitability for his lofty mission.

THOMAS THE CYNIC

Have you known him long?

PROFESSOR PICKUP

I've been working for him for a couple of years, and in spite of his terrible disposition, I've become sincerely fond of him. This makes it all the sadder for me to hear now and then from other people about certain episodes from his past which are far from encouraging. I mean, encouraging to his career.

THOMAS THE CYNIC

I don't know what you're alluding to. But I can tell you that things which might damage an archbishop's reputation are not necessarily of discredit to an aspiring dictator.

PROFESSOR PICKUP

From a former schoolmate of his, who turned up in this very hotel, I learned that he quit school to play the saxophone in a low dive in San Francisco. I had been unaware of that fact.

THOMAS THE CYNIC

I don't find it such a dishonorable occupation.

PROFESSOR PICKUP

It appears that he also composed some tangos and fox trots in the worst possible taste to appeal to the truck drivers and drunks in the place where he performed.

THOMAS THE CYNIC

You know, I think all of this might actually be in Mr. Double You's favor.

PROFESSOR PICKUP

What do you mean?

THOMAS THE CYNIC

Artistic aspirations, attempts at self-expression through writing, painting, music or some other art form, are to be found in almost all the biographies of great dictators. Failure as an artist, through lack of training or lack of taste, has been one of the most frequent and painful thorns in the dictator's side. Some dictators have taken an easy revenge, after seizing power, by forcing their subjects to admire their creations. Mind you, not only in modern times. It is said that Dionysius the Tyrant wrote tragedies so ridiculous that the poet Philomene couldn't keep a straight face while listening to them, even though he knew the severe punishment that awaited him for his crime of *lèse-majesté*. The same Dionysius bought the steel stylus with which Aeschylus had written his tragedies, in the belief that it would help him write in the same way. But the result was even more ridiculous.

PROFESSOR PICKUP

Then Mr. Double You would only be following tradition if, when he becomes dictator, he forces one of his fox trots on the United States as the new national anthem.

THOMAS THE CYNIC

There's no point in wasting time in recalling all

the details of Nero and his lyre, or how Napoleon Bonaparte, as a young officer unaware of his future, wasted his time writing a rhetorical *Dialogue sur l'Amour* and some *Réflexions sur l'état de nature*, a feeble imitation of the *Nouvelle Héloise*.

What we know of contemporary dictators is more instructive, because it reveals a part of their youthful mentality which is easier for us to follow in its later development. Hitler, as everyone knows, wanted to be a painter. At the age of eighteen he twice attempted the entrance exams for the Vienna Academy, and on both occasions his drawing was found poor and he was rejected. This failure depressed him enormously and he didn't dare reveal it to his mother at one time, nor did he mention it later in his autobiography, even though he describes many other events of less importance. This means that his failure to satisfy his artistic aspiration, which would have allowed him to climb the social ladder a rung or so higher than his family's condition, wounded him and left a scar that continued to ache for a long time afterward. This same resentment is probably at the bottom of the crusade against modern art which he undertook thirty years later, as soon as he reached power.

Our own Mussolini also attempted literature as a young man; in his case too, no doubt, it was partly in the hope of climbing the social scale, just as when he was a mere elementary school teacher, he had visiting cards printed saying PROFESSOR BENITO MUSSOLINI. His books have no esthetic value, but their psychological value is of decisive importance in understanding the mind of the young Mussolini. His masterpiece, so to speak, is an anticlerical-pornographic novel entitled *Claudia Particella ossia l'Amante del Cardinale (Clau-*

.

dia Particella, or the Cardinal's Mistress), which even Mussolini's official Fascist biographer, Margherita Sarfatti, defines as a "terrible mish-mash without head or tail, a kind of gaudy feature film, a dime novel." And these are euphemisms. In the same spirit as the *Amante del Cardinale*, Mussolini had conceived another novel, *La Lampada senza Luce* (*The Lamp without Light*), a story called *Vocazione* (*Vocation*), one drama entitled *Si comincia, Signori* (*Gentlemen, We Begin*), which takes place among hoodlums in the lower depths of the city, and another drama entitled *Reparto tranquilli* (*The Calm Ward*), which is set in an insane asylum. The theme of these writings, in all its clumsiness, is always the same: priests and nuns violating their vows of chastity, sadistic portrayals of deformities and vices and criminal passions; whereas the style recalls the bombastic prose of a provincial newspaper. But this didn't prevent Mussolini from becoming dictator in the land of Leopardi and Manzoni. The circumstances that made his success possible were obviously political and social, not esthetic. Yet it is extremely significant that, on the basis of these circumstances, a man with the mentality of the author of *Claudia Particella* should have proved the most suited to lead the Fascist movement. The future biographers of Mr. Double You will ask themselves: if our dictator had been a brilliantly successful sax player and composer of tangos and foxtrots, would he ever have had the idea of organizing a March on Washington?

PROFESSOR PICKUP

You're very entertaining, Mr. Cynic. Entertaining and paradoxical; there's no denying that. But this musical episode is only one of several; I mentioned it first because it's the freshest in my mind, not because I consider it the most serious. I don't know if you realize how bitter and personal American political attacks can be. Now, in a pamphlet recently published attacking Mr. Double You, along with a lot of nonsense, there are some alarming insinuations which, unfortunately, are not without a basis in fact.

THOMAS THE CYNIC

For example?

PROFESSOR PICKUP

They cast some doubt on his American origin. Mr. Double You himself was upset by this, and when I insisted that he should make his family tree public, he answered me in a rather vulgar way.

THOMAS THE CYNIC

If I haven't misunderstood you, my dear Professor, both he and you believe that a political leader must definitely be a native of the country in which he carries on his political activity.

PROFESSOR PICKUP

Of course. That's the least you can expect of a nationalist leader or of anyone who sings the praises of traditional values and demands a return to grass roots.

THOMAS THE CYNIC

Well, I'm happy to be able to reassure you on this point. I didn't know that Mr. Double You wasn't a pure American; but now I see that he fulfills a new requisite which makes him highly fitted to lead a nationalist and xenophobic movement in America. No doubt you're aware that Hitler, the most successful dictator of our time, was born at Braunau, in Austria. Only a few years before becoming Chancellor of the Reich, he narrowly escaped being thrown out of Germany as an "undesirable alien." Another contemporary dictator, Mustapha Kemal Ataturk, was born at Salonika. We don't know for sure whether he was an Albanian or a Macedonian, and yet he was dictator of Turkey. He, too, toward the end of 1922 was almost expelled from Turkey as a foreigner. Napoleon Bonaparte was a Corsican, something halfway between French and Italian, and he spoke badly the language of the country over which he ruled. This matter of foreign origin isn't a prerogative of rulers who achieve power through violence; it is even more frequent in the traditional forms of government. The royal families of England, Russia, Spain, Rumania and other countries all had German or Austrian origins. The Swedish dynasty descends from a Frenchman, a creature of Napoleon. Marriages among the various royal families have the result that none of them is without foreign blood, and yet the king is generally considered the purest and most genuine representative of his country, the living symbol of the ancient, innate virtues of his people. As for Mr. Double You, everything depends on the outcome of his struggle. If he wins, his biographers will have no trouble in proving that one of his ancestors landed with the Pilgrims on the *Mayflower*. I propose a toast, Professor, drink with me to the good health of the descendant of the *Mayflower*.

PROFESSOR PICKUP

And to America. But here comes Mr. Double You.

MR. DOUBLE YOU

I suppose you two have taken advantage of my absence to talk about me behind my back. Don't deny it.

PROFESSOR PICKUP

Your every failing has a peerless defender in Mr. Cynic. But, my friend, since you're looking more tired and pale than usual, I suggest you go straight up to your room.

MR. DOUBLE YOU

No, I hate being alone.

PROFESSOR PICKUP

Has the doctor at least prescribed a new remedy for your insomnia?

MR. DOUBLE YOU

I don't think there's anything left to try.

THOMAS THE CYNIC

You suffer from insomnia? Well, if it's any comfort to you to share an infirmity of great men, let me tell you that from Julius Caesar to Hitler all dictators suffered terribly from migraine before coming to power. This detail—on which all biographers agree— is highly important, because in the case of some of them it's the only proof that they had a head.

MR. DOUBLE YOU

Please continue the conversation that was interrupted by my arrival.

PROFESSOR PICKUP

Oh, we were just chatting idly.

THOMAS THE CYNIC

We did mention some qualities of the aspiring dictator.

MR. DOUBLE YOU

That's fine. Go right ahead.

PROFESSOR PICKUP

In all biographies of dictators I've always been particularly fascinated by the parts that tell of the years of waiting, the years of youth. You see the young man, predestined to become a dictator, passing his childhood and early manhood far from the noise of the crowd, in solitary places, lonely islands or mountain tops. If he occasionally goes to the city, it's only to visit the glorious monuments of the past, and when he finds them abandoned and falling to pieces, his rage is expressed in noble invective which always draws a crowd. But the vulgar herd doesn't understand him, the time is not yet ripe, and he is considered a poor dimwit.

MR. DOUBLE YOU

I share the opinion of the vulgar herd. Your description couldn't sound sillier.

PROFESSOR PICKUP

You're free to think that, if it helps you to excuse your own wasted youth. The rude way you speak to me, even in front of strangers, authorizes me—I believe—to answer you in the same tone. You tried your hand at five or six different trades, but you don't know any one of them well enough to make a position for yourself. You've always had great ambitions, but never the tenacity that a great ambition demands. You've always hated being alone, you always want somebody with you, but you've never been able to make any real friends. You're not lacking in certain good qualities, but so far you've never been able to adapt yourself to anything. During the war . . .

MR. DOUBLE YOU
Shut up.

THOMAS THE CYNIC
In such a personal argument, normally I'd have nothing to say. It would even have been painful for me to listen, and I would apologize, except that I overheard some details of Mr. Double You's early life which, so far as I can see, prove that he is cut from the same cloth as other dictators.

MR. DOUBLE YOU
What do you mean by that?

THOMAS THE CYNIC
One of the last statements of our illustrious professor could be quoted word for word as a definition of the childhood and youth of the aspiring dictator: he can never adapt himself to anything. I'm not referring to purely external difficulties—hunger, hostile surroundings, family misfortunes, illnesses. All these things are later described by the official biographers and become part of the legend; these misfortunes are much more frequent in ordinary life than most people

realize and many humble victims manage to overcome such troubles or adapt themselves to them. But the man who will one day be dictator can't adapt himself to anything. There are worse things than hunger. . . .

MR. DOUBLE YOU

There are many worse things than hunger.

THOMAS THE CYNIC

There is baseness, narrow-mindedness, boredom, sadness, doubt. But every now and then there is a painful, fleeting presentiment that something unheard of will occur and all the humiliations suffered will then be avenged. And meanwhile the months and the years go by, sluggishly, stupidly, sadly; friends and acquaintances settle down, become sensible, progress, buy a car, a house, marry, are honored and respected. The future dictator also tries his hand at something, but he can't adapt himself. He is still available for any enterprise of an extraordinary nature. A war, a political crisis, some form of social agitation will attract him, along with thousands of misfits like himself, just as a high tide draws off the flotsam along the shore. A bigger wave than the others will toss him up into full view on its crest. He is already another man: a leader. He himself will have no doubt that he was predestined by God, and he will adapt himself to this new role.

PROFESSOR PICKUP

Many biographers deny what you have stated.

THOMAS THE CYNIC

Courtiers always create a legend around any successful man. To distinguish reality from poetry, you have to know how to choose your texts. You probably know that the number of miracles attributed to Mahomet for the time he was alive increased from one century to the next. In the thirteenth century the number had already reached three thousand. He had had an extremely humble and difficult childhood; he had lost his father a few months before birth, and his mother when he was still a boy. But according to the legend his birth was heralded by portents, and from his first cries he revealed himself a prophet. Certain biographers and authors of fictionalized biographies today handle history like loyal Muslims.

PROFESSOR PICKUP

In a biography of Mussolini, which he himself presented me with, I read that when he was only a boy he heard inner voices saying "Rome, Rome," obviously alluding to the future March on Rome.

THOMAS THE CYNIC

He likes letting such things be told, but personally he has quite different memories of his childhood. He once said: "I never knew the serenity and the sweet tenderness of certain happy childhoods. Can you be surprised then that afterwards, in school, and to a certain extent, even now in mature life, I was— and am—harsh and reserved, touchy, almost savage? And yet my *real* story is all in those first fifteen years. My character was already formed then. I feel that those were my decisive influences. My whole future was already in me, in germinal form."

PROFESSOR PICKUP

In the days when he was a bricklayer, I read that Mussolini too worked here in Zurich.

THOMAS THE CYNIC

There are still some Italian Socialists here who remember him. To tell the truth, Mussolini was a bricklayer only in a manner of speaking. For a few days out of his life, he tried to work as a mason's helper, but he stopped at once and retained from those few days an indelible memory of physical labor. Those days were enough, though, for him to be called an ex-bricklayer. Those who knew him say that he was content to subsist on small relief allowances from socialist groups here.

PROFESSOR PICKUP

In *Mein Kampf* Hitler recalls how his talent as an orator was revealed to him as a child, when he used to argue with his schoolmates.

THOMAS THE CYNIC

Rather than arguments, they were bitter fights that broke into his habitual solitude. Resentment was a family inheritance in Hitler. His father had begun as a cobbler, but considered this trade humiliating. After struggles and privations, he succeeded in achieving the dearest dream of every Austrian: he became a civil servant. A civil servant of the lowest rank, but nevertheless a civil servant. He wanted his son to become a painter. At fourteen Hitler lost his father and suffered a lung ailment. After failing his high-school examinations, he spent the last two years of his mother's life at home in complete idleness.

As Hitler himself was to tell later, his father, before dying, considered Adolf a failure. Without talent as a painter and without the diploma necessary to enter a school of architecture, he was forced to become a draftsman. No contact with his fellow employees.

He tells how he drank his bottle of milk and ate his bread apart from the others. He observed his new surroundings with distrust and meditated on his wretched fate. When he was asked to join a trade union, he refused because he didn't want to admit he was a wage-earner, even though he was one.

From Germany let us skip to Turkey. The difference in the two countries' level of development is great, and the two dictatorships cannot be put in the same category. But now we are concerned with the formation of the aspiring dictator's personality. Armstrong, in his biography of Mustapha Kemal, says that Kemal's parents were poor but enterprising. The father was a humble clerk who in his free time engaged in various little business dealings. When his father died, Kemal was barely nine years old. The mother then retired to the country. Kemal was a silent, reserved boy; he rejected scoldings and punishments with bursts of rage; he had no friends. He was eleven when he was sent to high school at Salonika. There, because of his common manners, he was soon disliked by both teachers and schoolmates, and finally he was expelled. An uncle got him enrolled in the military academy. There too he made himself hated, though he was successful in his studies. He became boastful and unbearable; he couldn't stand anyone's surpassing him in studies; he hated and persecuted his rivals.

MR. DOUBLE YOU

I happened to be in Havana when the revolution led by the well-known Sergeant Fulgencio Batista broke out there. I was surprised to learn the story of that sergeant. At eleven, it seems, he was made apprentice to a tailor; then after that he was a waiter, a porter on Pullman cars, a locomotive engineer, and a day laborer on a sugar plantation. For many years— imagine!—his dream was to be a barber and own his own shop. But he wasn't able to achieve it. Instead he proved able to seize the government of Cuba. And Juan Vicente Gomez, before he terrorized Venezuela, was apparently a cowherd until he was thirty years old.

PROFESSOR PICKUP

My dear friend, we all know that in Latin America anything is possible. You mustn't forget, however, that even if your origin is a bit dubious, you are a citizen of the United States.

THOMAS THE CYNIC

We'll move on to more dignified examples. I'll just mention a few at random, since there's a wealth to choose from. The young Cromwell, future Lord Protector, is described by those who knew him as a person lacking in any grace, lacking in all talents which might serve to win the affection of those around him. In the years of his schooling in London, he was more outstanding as a football player and cudgel wielder than as a scholar. He was melancholy, nervous, at once timid and violent, and after giving up his studies he went through a dark period of depression and crisis, hesitating at the thought of any project. Napoleon Bonaparte didn't have an idyllic childhood. We all know the difficulties his mother had to overcome in bringing up her large family. As a student at Autun and at Brienne, the young Napoleon is described as solitary and taciturn, like so many other provincial boys at boarding school. His classmates teased him because of his odd appearance and because he was a Corsican. Proud and touchy, ambitious, without scruples, ready for any intrigue in order to get ahead—this is the portrait agreed on by all biographers before his meteoric rise began. Napoleon III had an eccentric, invalid father; he was brought up by his mother. His character was difficult and reserved, and his mother called him "the sweet gloomy one." He was filled with a great thirst for glory; his early manhood was tempestuous; he wandered in search of his fortune through many countries of Europe and America.

PROFESSOR PICKUP

But if these character defects were enough to make leaders, we'd have many more dictators than we have nations.

THOMAS THE CYNIC

Many are called, but fortunately few are chosen.

6.

Many are called, but few are chosen.

THOMAS THE CYNIC

In the Book of Judges there is a chapter on the *coup d'état* of Abimelech, the illegitimate son of Gideon, who hired and armed gangs of paupers and vagabonds to assist him in seizing power. With their assistance he slaughtered one by one and "upon one stone," as Scripture says, the seventy sons that Gideon had had by his lawful wives. The story of this misdeed is followed, in the same chapter, by a truly pitiless parable on the vocation of the political leader. This parable says that one day the trees, having decided to choose a king, went first to the olive and said, "Rule over us." But the olive said, "Do you want to force me to stop making oil and thus rendering honor to man and God according to my nature, to go hither and thither, always on the move, to be your leader?" Then the trees went to the fig tree and said "Come and be our ruler." The fig answered, "Would you have me forsake my sweetness and my good fruit and go forth into the streets of the world to concern myself with politics from morning till night?" Then the trees turned to the vine. "Come and rule over us," they said. And the vine also replied, "Would you have me stop making grapes, whose juice comforts man and God in sadness, in order to place myself at your head and waste time in idle chatter?" Finally the trees went to the bramble and proposed, "Come and rule us." And the bramble answered at once, "If your invitation to crown me king is sincere, come, my subjects, and rest in my shade; otherwise, may fire burst from my brambles and burn you all to ashes." This parable is undoubtedly one of the most subversive passages in the Bible. The bramble agrees to rule over the other trees because it has nothing better to do.

MR. DOUBLE YOU
Does that seem a poor reason to you?

PROFESSOR PICKUP
Not every crown is a crown of thorns.

MR. DOUBLE YOU
And what if it were?

THOMAS THE CYNIC
Well said, Mr. Double You. That answer does you credit. The nature of the true political man, compared to that of the ordinary man who is animated by a variety of interests and pleasures, can be considered like that of the bramble, which seems a sterile or ungenerous plant with respect to the others, but which is simply a different kind of plant—a plant, I would say, more self-centered. A man born with a political vocation cannot succeed in adapting himself to normal life, and sooner or later he will find his predestined way. As he pushes forward, everything else will become a matter of indifference to him and his vision will concentrate and focus on that single point, the sole source of his joys and sorrows. If there are any politicians who seek power so that they can carry out their ideas, as they say, or get rich, or possess women and thoroughbred horses, or for other such reasons, they are merely wretched intruders. The true political man wants power for power's sake; all voluptuousness lies, for him, in the exercise of power. Ideas, reforms,

peace, war, money, women, horses exist for him as instruments or objects of power, not the reverse. The men who now command in Rome, Berlin, Moscow— were they really extraordinary men, one wonders? People who knew them in their youth say no, and I can readily believe it. They were not at all exceptional, but I hasten to add that they were not commonplace either. The normal man is a chaos of desires; he likes to eat, drink, smoke, seduce women, raise canaries, play tennis, go to the theatre, wear good clothes, bring up children, collect stamps, have a profession and many other things. The normal man remains mediocre precisely because he can't resist frittering himself away in many and various desires. But the man with a true vocation for power dreams only of power. He is sentenced to power; it is his obsession, his trade, his family, his pastime. Since all his faculties are concentrated on this one point, to the masses he easily appears an extraordinary man, and thus becomes a leader. In the same way, those who concentrate completely on God become saints, and those who live only for money become billionaires.

PROFESSOR PICKUP

Is there any difference between what you call concentration on a single object and madness?

THOMAS THE CYNIC

The difference is in the quality of the object. In any case it is readily understandable that dictators, saints and millionaires seem inhuman to the ordinary man. Their behavior could never become a universal rule of life without transforming the world into a madhouse. The ordinary man's repugnance for such a

life is well depicted in the Biblical parable by the refusal of the olive, the fig, and the vine. Mind you,
they don't say that they don't want to rule, but that
they can't because, thank God, their nature is to be
useful and to lead an orderly life, not to be rushing
about, holding forth in the streets and giving themselves airs.

MR. DOUBLE YOU

Some people say Hitler and Mussolini are actual
madmen in the clinical sense of the word.

THOMAS THE CYNIC

I don't know about that, not being a psychiatrist.
But I've heard the way petty democratic and socialist
politicians argue in support of that diagnosis, and all
they say merely confirms their amateurish approach to
politics. The fascist leader's superiority over his opponents consists primarily in this: he aspires to power,
only power, and nothing else but power. Whether on
the side of the capitalists or the proletarians, the
priests or the devil, is a secondary matter; the important thing is power. This single-minded conception of
politics offers an unquestionable technical advantage
over the opposition, who are often good husbands and
fathers, sometimes even gentlemen, who have "ideas,"
"principles" and "programs," who are committed to
specific interests, who must answer for their behavior
before assemblies and congresses, and who, outside of
politics, have other pleasures such as reading, hunting,
fishing, music, golf, pipe-smoking, not to mention
the hobbies that provide so much copy for the illustrated magazines. To impose the totalitarian principle of the absolute priority of politics on an entire so-

ciety, the aspiring dictator must first of all be both incarnation and victim of that principle. In a word, for the totalitarian leader, politics isn't a career; it's an exclusive passion.

PROFESSOR PICKUP

Passion derives from the Latin *passio* and means suffering. Don't forget that, Mr. Double You.

THOMAS THE CYNIC

The Greeks had no doubts about the passionate nature of tyranny. In Plato's *Republic*, Socrates asks, "Perhaps it is for this reason that, since the most ancient times, Eros has been called a tyrant?" The very sadism of dictators obviously derives from Eros. During the proletarian revolt of the Ancona region in 1914, Mussolini wrote that he was recording these events "with the legitimate joy that the artist must feel at his own creation." He was then a militant member of the Socialist Party, but in this way of expressing himself he already revealed his latent Fascist vocation. In his war memoirs, Pilsudski confesses that in the first battles of the war he found much moving poetry, "as in one's first youthful love and one's first kiss." Even in *Mein Kampf*, which is frankly lugubrious, there is an exceptionally jolly passage where Hitler describes the first political meeting at which his stormtroopers beat their opponents to a bloody pulp. And to conclude, I'd like to recall a disclosure made by Stalin, a man who is usually taciturn and mistrustful. "There is really nothing more delightful," he once said to Kamenev, "than carefully plotting a trap into which your enemy in the party is bound to fall, and then going to bed."

PROFESSOR PICKUP

Do you think that the passion for an object is enough to enable one to possess it? I know many men who live only for money, but none of them has become a millionaire.

THOMAS THE CYNIC

I must repeat: the number of those called is always far greater than the number of those chosen.

PROFESSOR PICKUP

Well, let's forget about the herd of the called and concern ourselves with the little band of the chosen.

MR. DOUBLE YOU

So we can abandon the murky regions of psychology and get back to politics. Well, Mr. Cynic, how does this predestination come about?

THOMAS THE CYNIC

It isn't a single event, but a complex process. If you have time and if you're sufficiently interested, we can look into the main elements.

PROFESSOR PICKUP

May I say what I think about this? First of all, the aspirant must believe in himself. One November evening at Fontainebleau when Cardinal Fesch was deploring the arrest of Pius VII, Napoleon asked him if he noticed anything in the cloudy sky. And when the Cardinal said no, Napoleon replied: *"Eh bien, sachez donc vous taire: moi je vois mon étoile."* Henri de Saint-Simon, at fifteen, ordered his valet to wake him up every morning with the words "Get up, Monsieur le Comte, for you have great things to do." Later, Saint-Simon sent Louis XVIII a letter beginning "Prince, hear the voice of God, who speaks through my lips."

THOMAS THE CYNIC

Why did Count de Saint-Simon assign that curious morning reminder to his valet? It may be useful to look for the reason. Was he afraid of forgetting it perhaps? No, he could have written it on a piece of paper and nailed it beside his bed, or hung it on a string from the ceiling over his nose. The trick wouldn't have been so effective. The valet was necessary because, in a way, he represented society. "The greatness of the leader," Trotsky has written, "is a social quantity." The king presupposes subjects; the leader, followers. The Greeks rightly thought that it wasn't the tyrant who created slaves, but the slaves who created the tyrant. As in certain primitive forms of life, the subject is determined by the object: "It isn't the fish that takes the bait, but the bait, the fish." And similarly we may say that every nation, in the long run, gets the government it deserves. In fact, have free people ever been seen serving tyranny for any length of time, or servile people enjoying freedom? *Tyrannopoioi*, tyrant-makers, Plato called the demagogues who helped kindle the turbulent passions of youth; and he called a "tyrannic" generation one that caused moral and political disorder in the city, thus paving the way for the *coup d'état*.

MR. DOUBLE YOU

Your line of reasoning would be clearer if it had fewer adjectives.

THOMAS THE CYNIC

If the thing itself doesn't shock you, why should you be bothered by its color? Think it over carefully: the line of reasoning should please you. It should free you from any sentimental residue of personal inadequacy. From the moment when the spark is struck that identifies the leader with the masses the dictator feels his strength increase at a dizzying speed. Social identification is precisely that discriminatory process that causes the chosen to emerge from the flock of the called. The chosen one emerges transfigured. He loses his individual features and assumes the dream-personality of millions of his fellow citizens. He becomes literally the individualized product of an irresistible collective need. In today's mass civilization all the resources of technology contribute to the exaltation of the chosen man. A few of his compatriots may escape the general hypnosis and try to discuss and to denigrate him, recalling his origins, his lazy youth, his scanty culture, his cowardice, his inability to adapt himself to a normal life; but their work will be in vain because, for example, Fascism's present Duce, as he exists in the minds of many Italians and foreigners, has very little in common with the Signor Benito Mussolini of pre-war years. It was that Signor Mussolini, true enough, who founded the first *Fasci*, but then it was Fascism which in turn created the Duce, clothing his rather banal personality with all the virtues, defects and aspirations of the ego-ideal of millions of Italians. If you try to criticize the dictator or to discuss his person or his conduct "objectively" with an ordinary Italian, it's like saying to a pious old woman in church, "My good woman, don't you see that the statue of Saint Anthony you're kneeling before has no artistic value and it's just a vulgar thing made of papier-mâché?" The good woman would scratch your eyes out. If you criticize the leader in the presence of a believer, it is as though you were attacking the sublimated part of his own nature, from which he draws the consolation he needs to endure the hardships of his wretched existence.

It is precisely this close identification between leader and masses that creates the strong cohesion of totalitarian parties. Even if today the leader says and does the opposite of what he said and did yesterday, and orders massacres of innocents, what does it matter? The strongest tie between the leader and his people is neither ideological nor programmatical nor ethical. "If my leader behaves that way, he must have his own good reasons for doing so," the fascist or the communist thinks. And since he is convinced that, in his own life, the reason he didn't have the success he deserved is that he wasn't clever or unscrupulous enough, he is actually proud that "his" leader is so clever and strong and knows so well how to wipe out his adversaries. This is the source of the totalitarian leader's superiority over the democratic politician, whom the electors generally see every four or five years when the time comes for new elections, and whom they consider an outsider.

MR. DOUBLE YOU

This morning, purely out of curiosity, we asked various people we met in the street if they could tell us the name of the President of the Swiss Confederation. Only two were able to give us any answer at all, and only one was correct, since the other man got last year's President mixed up with this year's. The others replied with vague gestures, as if to say that we were really asking too much of them. What a funny country.

THOMAS THE CYNIC

But you mustn't think that the politicians here are inferior to others or that, with a suitable propaganda campaign, one of them couldn't become a demigod. For the present there's no need; business is good, neutrality pays, and there is reciprocal trust. The balance among the different cantons, languages and religions is well maintained. That's why the social identification of the masses with the leaders is still in the polytheistic phase in Switzerland.

7.

*Concerning the party of the
aspiring dictator.*

MR. DOUBLE YOU

In Rome we met a number of people belonging
to the ruling party: academicians dressed up like ad-
mirals, generals covered with medals like fish with
scales, monsignori perfumed with incense, and ladies
of the aristocracy who had a faint smell of mothballs.
On every side we were greeted with amused curiosity,
as if we were Redskins. Those who were kind enough
to invite us to a café or a restaurant never failed to
bring along in-laws and aunts with their respective
children, and they always granted us the honor of
paying for everyone. This isn't what I want to talk to
you about now, but I must confess that my followers
in America are of a different order. So how is it possible to lump us all together in the same definition?

THOMAS THE CYNIC

Don't be in such a hurry, I beg you. The poets
and the monsignori, the generals, the ladies and their
escorts will all come to you after you are in power.
With some exceptions, they flock to success like flies
to honey, or if you prefer, like rats to cheese. Democratic when there is a democratic government, they
are naturally fascists under a fascist dictatorship and
Communists under the hammer and sickle. The behavior of the priests might surprise us, if the pagans
hadn't already advised us that a winning cause has always pleased the gods. Christian theology later cor-
roborated this intellectually, explaining that all authority comes from God. And as for the ladies, it's well

known that Venus has always felt a particular attraction for Mars, the god of strength.

PROFESSOR PICKUP

On this score, I'm in complete agreement. But Mr. Double You hasn't said everything that's on his mind. He hasn't made his doubts clear. In reality, he not only lacks the support—as you well imagine—of those classes just mentioned that always follow the stronger side but also lacks anything that could be compared to the Fascist or National Socialist party before they came into power. It's true that the number of his followers increases every month, and there are already many who see in him "the man of tomorrow" and the "future dictator of America"; but he doesn't have a proper party behind him, a party like the one fascist literature describes—to distinguish it from others—as "a granite block of consciences and wills" and as a "cohort of iron consecrated to death" like a "single mind and a single body at the orders of a leader."

THOMAS THE CYNIC

I realize that you have formed a false picture of the origins and development of the Fascist party. If you examine closely the fluctuations of the internal composition of the Italian Fascist Party, for example, you can easily see that it changed radically at every phase of its stormy political development. The first *Fasci*, formed in the principal Italian cities in 1919, were made up almost entirely of former war volunteers, demobilized officers, disabled veterans, *arditi* and students. In 1920 the Fascist movement spread into the rural areas, thanks to the support of the great landowners and a number of peasants with small holdings. These peasants had grown rich during the war and were anxious to hang on to the privileges they felt were being threatened by both the day laborers and the factory workers. It was then that D'Annunzio defined Fascism as "an agrarian slavery movement." But in 1921 and 1922, after the failure of the Socialists' occupation of the factories, Fascism gradually won over the cities, one by one. Few workers joined, but there were numerous artisans, small businessmen and industrialists, technicians, the unemployed, and the misfits without any fixed occupation. In 1923, after the March on Rome, the Fascist party was invaded by the bureaucrats, by the workers and skilled technicians employed by the great public concerns, and by provincial politicians from the defeated bourgeois parties. Finally, in 1925, according to Mussolini, the Fascist party was renovated from top to bottom, because of discontent with the government's economic and fiscal policy and the uneasiness that many Fascists evinced during the Matteotti crisis. In five years, from 1919 to 1925, the social composition of the Italian Fascist Party was profoundly modified a good five times.

The German National Socialist party had to face far more complex, tumultuous, and lengthy internal difficulties before it came to power. In the first nuclei which, from early 1919 to halfway through 1921, were formed by the Deutsch-Soziale Partei in Nuremberg, there were officers of the Freie-Korps, journalists, physicians, bankrupt artisans, clerks, students, and even a few workers who were rebelling against the organizations of their class. The Bavarian separatist leagues were then numerically stronger and were a decisive influence in turning the NSDAP into a party of the dissatisfied urban middle class. So it remained even after the end of July 1921, when Hitler had liquidated the party's founders and set himself up as Führer. The NSDAP developed numerically in 1922 and '23 even outside of Bavaria, but until its miserably unsuccessful putsch in November 1923 its antiparliamentary tactics and its renunciation of new *coups de main* allowed the National Socialist Party to put itself, for a while, at the head of the peasant classes, which had profited hugely from inflation and were therefore dissatisfied with the conservative parties, which had brought inflation to an end. In North Germany, where the NSDAP had previously been banned, the Deutschvölkische Partei caught on among the officer class and the landowners, and a good part of its membership was later to pass directly to the National Socialists. At the end of 1924, while Hitler was in prison because of the previous year's putsch, the NSDAP underwent a grave crisis, split into two groups, and lost the majority of its members. The economic situation of the following year, culminating in the American loans to Germany, marked the end of National Socialist influence in rural areas. From 1925 to 1929 Hitler had to rebuild his party on virtually new foundations—exploiting whatever was offered him: in the Rhineland, following Gregor Strasser and Goebbels, many ruined small merchants and also groups of unemployed workers; in the East, behind Otto Strasser, a number of deserters from the Social-Democrats and the Communists; following the Deutsch-Nazional leader Stoehr, head of a white-collar organization, many of this class; through the absorption of the so-called Bund der Artamanen, a certain number of young unemployed peasants; landowners in Pomerania and other regions; and in all the university cities, vociferous groups of students, for whom the prospect of a degree was coupled with the foreknowledge of certain unemployment.

When the Great Depression of 1929 took place, the NSDAP had a solid base for its gigantic later development. The ruined small businessmen immediately formed the nucleus of the urban organization, flanked by an ever-increasing number of white-collar workers and professional men, categories severely overpopulated in those years. During 1930, the NSDAP managed to take command of the peasant movement in various regions, especially in North Germany, inflaming to boiling point the feelings of revolt that had been growing there for some time. On the other hand, the National-Socialist influence among the industrial proletariat suffered many ups and downs, since it was hotly fought by the Communist party. Still the NSDAP had unquestionable successes between 1929 and 1930 among the workers in Saxony, Thuringia, Mecklenburg, and Baden. In the competition between the two demagogies, it looked as if the National Socialists were also having success among the unemployed workers of Berlin, but its advantage was partly lost in June 1930 when conflict broke out between Otto Strasser and Hitler. Strasser's extremist program then seemed sacrificed to the promises Hitler had made to the big industrialists. But the ineffectual policy of the Moscow-inspired rival party came to Hitler's aid, giving him every year a growing number of proletarian supporters, disappointed in their hopes of a socialist revolution and ready to fight for any ersatz form of it, merely to be fighting. But that's enough of this for now. I hope I've convinced you that the images of the "granite block" and the "co-

hort of iron," though they may be frequent in official Fascist literature, do not correspond in the least
to reality. But to resume the discussion at the point
where Mr. Double You began it, I must say that I
don't yet understand what sort of followers he has.

PROFESSOR PICKUP

To sum it up in a few words, and without meaning to hurt Mr. Double You's feelings, they are people
of no importance, often not even respectable. Apart
from some poor students and a few army men, personal friends from the European war and the days of
the Bonus March, at his rallies I've met malcontents of
every class: bankrupt merchants, unemployed workers, more or less hysterical women, farmers ruined by
taxes or mortgages. Frankly speaking, at times I had
the feeling I was at a meeting of the Salvation Army.
Mind you, what bothers me isn't the humble social
origin of most of Mr. Double You's followers (weren't
Christ's twelve apostles fishermen?), it's their lack of
discipline, the disorder of their minds, their vulgarity.
You can think what you like about authoritarian regimes, but you can't deny that they represent the restoration of the strict principles of hierarchy and social order. To tell you the truth, lately I've been making an effort to attract some people of superior quality into Mr. Double You's ranks: university professors,
artists, gentlemen . . .

THOMAS THE CYNIC

Be on your guard, Mr. Double You. Don't clutter
up your following with these pretentious, base people
that your adviser would like to attract to you. They
can come later, but not now. It's quite true that a

totalitarian movement, after it has seized power, becomes a party of order, or rather, *the* party of order.
But before reaching that point, it must be—to an extreme and implacable degree—the party of disorder.
You are still in the phase where you have to fish in
troubled waters. So don't be ashamed of your present
followers. Thanks to them, your movement is following the rule of Nazi and Fascist experience, in the
great tradition of the dictatorial parties of all times.
Surely you haven't forgotten what Professor Pickup
himself recalled a few days ago about the tyrannies of
ancient Greece.

PROFESSOR PICKUP

If you put it that way, I have to agree with you.
Another piece of democratic nonsense, in my opinion, is the belief that tyranny has always come from a
conspiracy of the upper classes of society against the
people. On the contrary, the ancient tyrants, even
when they themselves were not of plebeian origin, always counted on the plebs and had to fight against the
aristocracy. And it's the same, more or less, with
every other authoritarian power.

THOMAS THE CYNIC

For a very simple reason. Disagreements between
the tyrannic government and the upper classes always
originated from the fact that the latter, in the given
situations, were the only force capable of checking
the tyrant's whims. Thus the history of absolutism is
characterized by a permanent antagonism between the
monarch on one side and the Pope, bishops and barons
on the other, while the middle class concerned itself
only with business. Since it is in the most backward

situations that social phenomena are usually to be observed in their simplest form, nothing is more instructive in this connection than the story of Ivan the Terrible, in the chaotic period of his reign after the wars
against Livonia and Poland. Then Ivan was able to
exploit the popular hatred of the boyars, whom he
didn't trust, and with elements chosen from the people he created the *oprichina*, a forerunner of the modern OGPU. Four thousand boyars were executed, and
of those whose lives were spared many were expro-
priated.

Obviously the relationship between the totalitarian party and the masses is another matter. We come
closer to our own situation if we recall the movement
that supported Louis Bonaparte in his *coup d'état*. As
I read to you the masterful description that Marx has
left us in his *18 Brumaire* of the "Society of the 10th
of December," you will smell the morning air of our
own times. Please pay strict attention:

> With the pretext of founding a charitable organi-
> zation, the dregs of Paris had been organized into
> secret cells; each cell was directed by Bonapartist
> agents, the supreme leader was a Bonapartist gen-
> eral. Along with ruined gallows-birds who lived
> on ambiguous incomes and came from God
> knows where, along with the blacksheep off-
> spring of the bourgeoisie, there were vagabonds,
> penniless soldiers, ex-convicts, escaped galley-
> slaves, swindlers, clowns, wastrels, cutpurses, ma-
> gicians, porters, pimps, minstrels, ragpickers, knife-
> grinders, tinkers, beggars, in short the wandering,
> fluctuating, indeterminate mass that the French
> call *la bohème*. With this element, with which he

had so many affinities, Bonaparte formed the nucleus of the "Society of the 10th of December." A charitable society? Yes, in the sense that all its members, like Bonaparte, wanted to benefit themselves at the expense of the working nation. This Bonaparte, who makes himself Leader of the scum, who finds there, in a larger degree, the same personal interests that he is pursuing, who recognizes in these human dregs, the refuse of all classes, the only class on which he can absolutely depend, this is the true Bonaparte, the Bonaparte without high-flown slogans. . . . Members of this society, crammed into freight cars, provided a portable public on his travels, represented public enthusiasm by shouting "Long live the Emperor," insulted and clubbed the republicans—all this, naturally with police protection.

Here endeth Marx.

A modern totalitarian movement is naturally different in many respects from the Bonapartist movement, especially in the social structure and problems at stake. But in Italian Fascism of 1919-21 you could see many elements identical with those of the "Society of the 10th of December." Along with the students, the ex-officers, the ex-*arditi* without work and without a civilian profession, there were many hoodlums and professional criminals, especially in the urban *Fasci*.

MR. DOUBLE YOU

Are Italian criminals so prone to follow the advice of the authorities?

THOMAS THE CYNIC

They didn't offer their services free. The criminal who agreed to place himself at the *Fascio's* disposal was immediately free from surveillance and from the prohibition to change his residence, and received a financial reward for every patriotic crime that he could make himself guilty of. But apart from that, I'd say the hoodlum spontaneously tends towards reactionary sentiments; he is repelled by the proletarian situation from which he has escaped; and he hopes, thanks to a lucky job, to become a *rentier*.

MR. DOUBLE YOU

As far as the use of criminals in political conflicts is concerned, I hope you'll forgive me if I say, all modesty aside, that on that score we American have nothing to learn from you Europeans.

THOMAS THE CYNIC

The fascist movement's originality lies in the fact that even though many of its cells are formed with the connivance of the rich—the military authorities and the political police, who secretly or openly intend to exploit the fascists and then get rid of them—the movement nevertheless rapidly achieves an independent political life, passes the limits that its benefactors would like to set for it, and finally announces its candidacy for the control of the State. The secret of this good fortune of a fascist party is essentially in the place it occupies in society, between a governing class helpless to cope with the new needs of the country and an opposition incapable of taking its place. To occupy that place in the most profitable way and to seize fortune by the horns, the fascist party must be led by a man desperately anxious to succeed, a born rabble-rouser, having at his disposal a mass of beggars, failures, misfits, bullies, a mob which has mutinied against the ruling class and against the traditional parties, including the so-called revolutionary ones, a mob, finally, that has been through the war and is familiar with death. I think that, in our time, when such a party is formed, it has many chances of success.

MR. DOUBLE YOU

Your optimism doesn't completely convince me, but it encourages me.

8.

Concerning the uselessness of political programs, the danger of discussions, and the modern technique of swaying the masses.

MR. DOUBLE YOU

Shall we talk today about political programs?

THOMAS THE CYNIC

Gladly. I hope to succeed in convincing you not to take them too seriously.

PROFESSOR PICKUP

Are you going to start again with those anti-intellectual prejudices of yours?

THOMAS THE CYNIC

If I'm to give sincere advice to an aspiring dictator, they're inevitable. I admit that in a healthy political life competition between the parties would take the form of their presenting opposing political and economic programs. But fascism is born in an entirely different atmosphere. Of course, it makes immediate claims, with all kinds of slogans, to win the support of the social forces that it needs; but apart from that it is careful not to formulate a constructive program. In its stead, fascism proposes an ideology formed of symbols of race or nation. If you are aiming at success, Mr. Double You, you must follow this rule: throw discredit on the traditional party system and on politics itself, make them responsible for all the nation's ills and rouse the hatred of the masses against them.

PROFESSOR PICKUP

I should think those methods would fool only the most backward part of the nation.

THOMAS THE CYNIC

What do you mean by "backward," in the age of mass civilization? The apparent refinement of the middle and upper classes shines in normal times, but it is only a varnish that cracks the moment the situation becomes desperate. Leftovers of primitive mentality, pre-logical and a-logical, are in wait on every rung of the social ladder.

PROFESSOR PICKUP

What you consider leftovers of primitive mentality, Mr. Cynic, are really the inexhaustible springs of religious feeling. From my point of view, the misunderstanding of this most noble part of man's spirit, and the vulgar materialism adopted as doctrine were, beyond doubt, the causes of the miserable fate of European socialism.

THOMAS THE CYNIC

If you'll allow me, we'll talk about religion perhaps on some other occasion. As far as socialism is concerned, you must admit that its defeat was not metaphysical but all too physical. You can't understand the victory of the fascist mystique over socialist "materialism" unless you realize that it meant the apparent elimination of a certain number of vital problems which socialism, for better or for worse, represented and the substitution for them of vague phrases and "states of mind." Those problems, however, were not arbitrary, they hadn't been invented by the socialists, and therefore they remain at the base of the general disorder of society and have a weighty influence on fascism itself. The only way to eliminate concrete problems is to solve them, not to ignore or to disguise them. On the other hand, we must admit that the socialists, concentrating on the class struggle and traditional politics, were surprised by the savage way fascism burst on the scene. They couldn't understand the motives or the consequences of fascism's verbiage and strange symbols, and they couldn't even imagine that such a primitive movement could gain control of such a complicated machine as the modern state and, what's more, hold on to it. The socialists were incapable of understanding the efficiency of fascist propaganda, because their doctrine had been formulated by Marx and Engels in the last century and hadn't progressed since then. Marx couldn't foresee the discoveries of modern psychology, nor the forms and political consequences of today's mass civilization.

MR. DOUBLE YOU

The philosopher Huizinga, whom we visited in Holland, told us that the illness of our civilization is the weakening of our critical sense and logical processes. There is a conflict between life and religion, he told us, and modern youth worships life. As a philosopher, he naturally spoke of this with bitterness. But if that's the way things are, as even you cynically agree, why shouldn't a political leader take advantage of the situation?

THOMAS THE CYNIC

Your question, Mr. Double You, is beyond the established limits that make our conversations possible.

We are supposed to concern ourselves with the *how* and not with the *why*.

MR. DOUBLE YOU

I don't understand the difference, but you may continue.

THOMAS THE CYNIC

Now, on the subject of the *how*, I must repeat that in Italy first and then in Germany the fascists began to get the upper hand at the moment when the socialist parties revealed themselves unable to fulfill the hopes that the masses had placed in them. Just as a private individual, when helpless to overcome the difficulties of his life and to achieve his aspirations, releases his anxieties and desires in dreams, so the masses, when the incapacity of their leaders causes their defeat, try to escape their own despair, taking refuge behind the emblems of a distant age in which social contradictions are "symbolically" resolved, men are "symbolically" brothers, and capitalist profits are "symbolically" eliminated.

PROFESSOR PICKUP

Do you really believe that in the fascist ideology of European countries fiction has such an important role?

THOMAS THE CYNIC

In every ideology and in every kind of state, my dear Professor, but in a special way, obviously, in totalitarian states. The English anthropologist Frazer once stated that the maintaining of public order and the state's authority has always been essentially based on the superstitious images that the masses form of it. Without these images, in fact, much of history would remain incomprehensible. Wars would be incomprehensible, the existence of parasitical social classes would be incomprehensible, and so would barracks, prisons, the relationship between colonies and metropolises, and all the rest. No, fascism really didn't fall from the blue, and it subjugated not free men, but crowds already prepared to serve by their way of daily life and already trained to obey by all the forms of democratic society (teaching in schools, military service, religious practices, and even by the training received in the trade unions and opposition parties, which were centralized and bureaucratized like everything else). The psychologist Bernheim claimed that the human spirit has an innate tendency to accept hypnotic suggestion and that the normal brain is stocked prevalently with "a series of hypnotically-induced ideas." The existence of an atavistic disposition towards hypnotic suggestion in man does not exclude the possibility of overcoming it to make room for a free and responsible consciousness. But this fact is disagreeable to most politicians, who like to use men as obedient instruments. And it can be a painful fact for the ordinary man too. The life of domestic animals may not always be enviable, but it's often the only way to live in peace.

PROFESSOR PICKUP

Are you trying to violate human nature, Mr. Cynic? Please don't forget that freedom of conscience has always been the privilege of a restricted elite and it presupposes a richness of thought which the masses could never possess. The masses can receive their spiritual nourishment only in the form of pills—to be swallowed with eyes closed.

THOMAS THE CYNIC

If anything, history proves the contrary. It proves that there has been no political or social progress of any importance that wasn't due to the struggles of the so-called lower classes. But let's not stray too far from our theme: I want now to insist on the fact that education, even higher education, isn't at all incompatible with credulity and superstition. I know a famous professor of mathematics who trembles if he encounters a black cat on his way to the university. The most dangerous superstitions are the ingrained ones, which we aren't even aware of as such. I would never have noticed many of them myself if a friend of mine from Papua hadn't pointed them out to me. I'd like to tell you his story if you don't mind.

A missionary chanced to take him from one of the most backward tribes of Dutch New Guinea and had him sent to Rome, to the seminary of the Propaganda Fide. There he was to be freed from his native superstitions and given a Christian education. Though he had a quick mind, he never made any objections to the truths of the gospel, and he seemed already mature enough to be sent back to his own tribe as a native missionary, when chance or Providence caused him to visit the zoo of the Eternal City and come upon a magnificent old kangaroo. The kangaroo was and is the totem animal of that young man's original tribe, and you can't imagine his emotion in discovering his sacred ancestor in that foreign city. He had no doubt that the kangaroo had arrived there by supernatural means to warn him not to forget his origins and to remain faithful to his forefathers. His Catholic teachers tried to free their young convert from that belated access of superstition, bringing to bear all the forces of Christian apologetics. Their efforts were in vain. Finally they cast the impenitent pagan out of the seminary, where he had become an occasion of scandal. He wandered, sad and dejected, from city to city, and eventually he came to Switzerland. I happened to make his acquaintance in the Zurich zoo, as he was strolling around, full of excitement, in the kangaroo section. When I showed him that I was somewhat familiar with recent studies of the mythical world of the Australian and Papuan tribes, he began to rave.

"I've read these scientists of yours," he protested, "and they're all fools. In their pretentious writings, they go on about our *alchera, ungud, Kugi, dema,* as if they were inanimate laboratory objects." Highly agitated, he took a notebook from his pocket and insisted that I read it. "Here is my revenge," he said. On the cover of the notebook a title was written: *The Incredible Superstitions of the European Tribes.* I must confess that I read the notebook in one sitting. The young Papuan, with his virgin eyes, had managed to discover an incredible number of fetishes, idols, totems and tabus which dominate the most important actions of our daily life, almost— I might add—without our being aware of it. The notebook was written in anecdotal form, recording the discoveries in the order in which they had been made. As you can imagine, the entire Catholic liturgy, with its incense, candles, lamps, oils, ashes, relics, occupied the place of honor. But there was no dearth of bizarre observations of our private life. I particularly remember a discussion between the Papuan and a Roman woman who wore a little golden ring, her wedding ring, on her finger. I should explain that the Italian word for wedding ring is *fede,* which can also mean either *fidelity* or *faith.* This multiple meaning involved my Papuan friend in a somewhat confusing conversation. Starting with questions about the functions of that wedding ring, the young man went on to the relationship between it and marital fidelity, the institution of the *Propaganda Fide* (Propagation of the Faith) and the offer of wedding rings to the Fascist Fatherland when it needed gold. At a certain point the woman was unable to answer any more of his questions. One day, along with the other clerics of his college, the Papuan was taken to Rome's Piazza Venezia, to pay homage to the Tomb of the Unknown Soldier which, as you may know, is located at the foot of the "Altar of the Fatherland." "Is the Fatherland also a Madonna?" he asked one of his superiors. "No," the older man answered. "Then why is there an altar to it?" "You wouldn't understand." "Why not?" Two policemen came up and made them be silent. "If I have to be silent, that means there's a Madonna around," the Papuan went on muttering. Another day he noted in his book: "I read in a newspaper that in Ethiopia the Roman wolf has driven out the Lion of Judah. And apparently the British lion betrayed the Judah one. So, just as we do at home, every great European tribe venerates a totem ancestor: France has the cockerel, Germany the eagle, Italy too has an eagle, whereas Rome has a she-wolf with two babies, Holland, Belgium, Sweden and other countries have the lion, the most frequently venerated animal in Europe." Another time, in Genoa, he witnessed the launching of a ship. A lady broke a bottle against the hull. They explained to him that this was a bottle of champagne. "Too bad," he said, "it would be better to break a bottle of water and drink the champagne." "The baptism wouldn't be valid," he was told. "But wasn't Jesus baptized with water?" he answered. "You're stupid," they replied. The argument went on. "Does a ship have a soul?" he asked. "No," they said. "What has been baptized then?" Again they answered: "You're stupid." Another day he saw many men marching by, all dressed in the same way. In front of them walked a man holding a stick with a scrap of colored cloth attached to it. An old man who didn't take off his hat was immediately attacked and clubbed. "Why?" the Papuan asked. "He didn't salute the flag," was the explanation. "But it's only a piece of cloth," he observed. A hulking fellow shouted and shook his fist at the Papuan: "The flag is the sacred image of the Fatherland." "It's the Fatherland itself," another one shouted, "it's the blood, the soul of the Fatherland." "Has the Fatherland a soul?" the Papuan asked. They wanted to take him to prison. A number of further episodes recorded in the notebook are concerned with the magic power of rubber stamps, uniforms, badges. They are things that we all know, but because of habit, we pay no attention to them.

MR. DOUBLE YOU

Your little story is amusing, but I don't see what connection it has with our conversation today.

THOMAS THE CYNIC

The connection is obvious. In a study by the ethnographer A. P. Elkins of the secret life of the Australian aborigines, I found the following opinion. The tie between an individual and his country is not simply geographical or fortuitous; it is a vital, spiritual and holy bond. His country is the symbol of access to the invisible and powerful world of the heroes, of his ancestors, and of the powers that grant life, by which man and nature flourish. I warned you that I was talking about Australian aborigines, to keep you from thinking that A. P. Elkins was quoting the slogans of German National Socialist propaganda. Still there is a difference between the spiritual attitudes of the two peoples—entirely to the advantage of the Australian aborigines. In them that mythic contact with the forces of nature is still spontaneous and pure; in today's Germans it's the influence of hazy ideologies, whose success lies in the terrible spiritual confusion of the German people during the post-war years.

MR. DOUBLE YOU

No matter how clever it is, a propaganda campaign can't succeed unless it has some link with reality. But in America we lack traditions. Our history begins with the Declaration of Independence in the year 1776. Before then the thirteen states were English colonies. So our brief history is all liberal. If you reflect a moment on the fact that in 1776 the United States had barely two million inhabitants (and a certain number of the most distinguished families left the country then and went back to England) and that the inhabitants now number 130 million, you will see clearly that from a purely demographic point of view, the United States is a creation of the liberal epoch, a recent creation. In such circumstances you can't invent a national tradition.

THOMAS THE CYNIC

Do you visualize the Italians of today as nurturing the traditions of Ancient Rome? Don't delude yourself. A few years ago some Italian historians were arguing about the period in which the origin of their nation should be set. Some wanted to establish it as the beginning of the 1800's, others in the 1700's. Some went as far back as 1300 and Dante. But nobody, not even a Fascist historian—and with the Fascists in power there is, needless to say, no lack of Fascist historians—dared assert that Italian history went back to classical antiquity. This didn't prevent Mussolini from inflating that historical nonsense about Italy's Roman tradition until he had made it the central myth of Fascist ideology, exploiting it for the titles, symbols and rites of the party organization and the Fascist state. In large areas of public opinion the mystification seems to have succeeded. There have been young men who went as volunteers to Africa and Spain, consecrating their faith in the Roman tradition with their blood.

MR. DOUBLE YOU

For a mystification to succeed, the way I look at it, it must have at least some semblance of truth. Between the Italy of today and the Rome of the Caesars, there is at least a geographical coincidence. In America we don't have any equivalent.

THOMAS THE CYNIC

Don't despair. To bring off a mystification, the first requirement is that the people to be mystified should have the necessary receptivity. A French scholar has written that a myth is the personification of a collective desire. To get a hypnotic process going, content is of secondary importance; the mental state of the person to be hypnotized is the decisive factor. One might sum it up by saying that every successful hypnotic process is ultimately self-hypnosis. This is the answer to those who, after meeting the Fascist and National Socialist leaders in person and sizing up their intellectual and moral limitations, cannot understand how such mediocre men could possibly have created such powerful mass movements. Actually the men in question did not create those formidable movements; they merely reap their profits. So the secret of National Socialism and Fascism must be sought primarily in the mood of the Italian and German masses after the war, the economic crisis, and the failure of the democratic and socialist parties.

MR. DOUBLE YOU

Let's not forget the purpose of our conversations, if you don't mind. What conclusions do you intend to draw from what you've been saying?

THOMAS THE CYNIC

The most important conclusion is this: don't be discouraged. Don't think that the aspiring dictator's task is to create a dictatorship out of nothing. Instead you should pin your hopes to the incapacity of traditional parties to overcome this crisis of civilization which seems to have overtaken the whole of humanity. Don't forget that in all probability we are only at the beginning of a long series of wars, revolutions, counter-revolutions, disasters of every kind. Don't be in a hurry. Have faith in the possible rebarbarization of humanity. Even without a great historical tradition behind them, the masses can still become barbarians again, with the efficient help of war, hunger, the radio, and all the rest of it. God forbid that I should cast doubt on the wisdom of Professor Pickup and your other collaborators; and yet, to get the masses thoroughly stupefied the efforts of the best propagandists would be as harmless as the buzzing of flies, were it not for the decisive collaboration of wartime holocausts and unremitting poverty. Please don't be shocked if I call things by their name; I avoid paraphrases for the sake of clarity. It's now an established fact that in the wake of international wars, civil wars and long periods of unemployment, there is an epidemic of what might be called "disintegrated consciousness," as a result of which an ever-increasing number of people are deprived of their normal mental activity. They suffer a gradual atrophy of the spirit and a hypertrophy of the lower mental faculties, the instinctive and automatic ones. I don't mean the serious cases which require psychiatric treatment, but in general, the mass of veterans and unemployed, their families, all those who are subjected for a long time to intense emotions. Except for unusual cases, experience proves that in these painful trials the human spirit loses its habitual equilibrium, is no longer capable of reasoning and reflecting, wavers between black despair and naïve optimism, and becomes the easy prey of any demagogue. A state of physical danger, combined with that of not knowing where one's next meal is going to come from, if it lasts for years, will lead even the most normal, most cultivated, even the most well-bred man, back to a situation of primitive anxieties, to a stage which, after so many centuries of development, seemed to have been left behind for good.

This is the psychological moment when the totalitarians take over—not the parlor totalitarians but the real ones, the desperate ones, whose very appearance in a public place is enough to strike terror into people's hearts.

MR. DOUBLE YOU

What you're saying now, Mr. Cynic, reminds me of something that the Spaniard Ortega y Gasset told us when we met him in Paris. Any man who begins to rule now, he said, is a primitive, a barbarian, a man from nowhere, a vertical invader, compared to the complex civilization from which he comes. His personality is rudimentary; he is capable of acting only in a group. In a word, he is a mass-man. But this is a commonplace by now.

PROFESSOR PICKUP

Fascism's mobilization of millions of mass-men, however, is not the whole of fascism. The essence of fascism is in its idea. The mass-man is the brute strength which the idea uses in order to triumph. Behind Mussolini are Sorel, Pareto, the Roman tradition. Behind Hitler, Fichte with his National Socialism, Nietzsche's *Willen zur Macht*, Richard Wagner's faith in destiny, the racial theories of Gobineau and Houston Stewart Chamberlain, Mendel's law of heredity, Treitschke's idea of power. . . .

MR. DOUBLE YOU

Would you please stop it? Why do you insist on making us waste time? You know perfectly well that in America ideas are not allowed to circulate outside the universities, and in political life least of all.

PROFESSOR PICKUP

Ah, my friend, this is the very misfortune which must be brought to an end. The bombastic liberal and Christian tradition must be replaced—the next social crisis will demonstrate its impotence—by a new, simple, modern idea, which can arouse the support of the young intellectuals and sway millions of mass-men. So the first task is to open a discussion. . . .

THOMAS THE CYNIC

May I interrupt you? You're on the wrong track. I mean, the path you plan to follow will not lead to fascism. You want to open a discussion? Fascism, in reality, is the attempt to place the social order beyond all discussion, to make it independent of the citizens' conscience and the fluctuations of public opinion. For fascism, society is eternal; it is already there when man is born, and it continues to exist after he dies. Man must adapt himself to society, and not vice versa. In this sense European fascism is an attempt to move the relationship between man and society back to where it was two centuries ago. Forgive my pedantry. You know, of course, that up to the Enlightenment, the problem of social organization as a whole had never been questioned. But with the Enlightenment society itself became a problem. Then began the period of political and social theorizing, the period of programs. Liberalism was born, and with it all the varieties of democracy and socialism, each of them representing a different way of conceiving human relationships. It looked as if reason had definitely unseated tradition. But all this happened in a purely abstract realm. Society in the last century continued to flourish and to evolve, while obeying laws other than those of reason. This development itself, however, became a subject of discussion, giving rise to more new programs; and, to tell the truth, nobody saw any harm in it. Finally the World War created a situation in which discussion became dangerous. The old social order proved to be rationally indefensible. And then fascism was born. Must I summarize what we have already said at our previous meetings? It was born from the anxiety of the middle classes, who saw their existence threatened by technical progress; from the disillusionment of the workers bruised by their defeat in badly organized attempts at revolution; from the fear of the capitalists at the looming menace of expropriation and social death. Fascism didn't come forward with a counter-program to the programs already in existence; it didn't even criticize the programs of its opponents; it grew up at a remove from all notion of discussion, denying that society might be a topic for argument. Fascism appealed, against the "disruptive quibbling of politicians," to primitive instincts, to the call of the blood, tradition, the mystique of the herd, danger, "safety in obedience," the "chastity of sacrifice," brotherhood dictated by destiny. To anything you like, but not to reason.

MR. DOUBLE YOU

In simpler terms, this is how I look at the thing insofar as it concerns me personally. If we have a worsening of the economic situation and of international relations simultaneously, it's probable that our two big parties will fold up. The motto "Down with politics" will then be very popular even in our country, and it will appeal to everybody: workers, farmers, and even the trusts. I don't mind confessing to you that I feel my political future depends on a situation like that. But then I ask myself: will it all be a flash in the pan? You see, there aren't many Americans who sincerely love politics or who would fight to defend the two-party system; but they all like freedom.

THOMAS THE CYNIC

Before Fascism took over in Italy, many people insisted that it was incompatible with our individualistic temperament. When it came to Germany, there was the same talk of incompatibility, and Hitler's primitive concepts were contrasted with the great German contributions to art and philosophy. With a formula which might have been borrowed from our own Professor Pickup's pantautology, up to 1933 you could hear people saying, "Germany isn't Italy," and then from 1933 to 1938, "Austria isn't Germany." You must bear in mind that even the most solid national tradition is represented, in the psychological stratification of the average individual, by completely superficial elements, which are the first to disappear in circumstances of extreme distress. No country has a national tradition or temperament that makes totalitarianism inevitable, but neither does it have one that makes it *a priori* impossible. National temperament plays a purely decorative role in the genesis of totalitarianism; it can be useful in distinguishing German Fascism from Jewish (yes, that exists, too), Italian Fascism from French or Irish. But mass civilization tends, in any case, to standardize national temperaments, whereas it doesn't even scratch atavistic complexes. These, being the remnants of an epoch when nations didn't exist, are to be found even in people without any national tradition at all, and most probably these complexes will go on existing when today's nations have disappeared. C. G. Jung, a psychoanalyist who lives in this city, discovered that Negroes dream about the same things as Europeans or Indians.

MR. DOUBLE YOU

Mr. Cynic, have you ever heard of our "log cabin and hard cider campaign" of 1840? A man with a romantic soul and no political program captured the most motley crowds by moving miniature log cabins on wheels and barrels of apple cider from one part of the country to another.

PROFESSOR PICKUP

My friends, we're off the track again. The relationship between leader and masses in the various regimes needs further elucidation. The casual contempt of the old politicians was expressed in the formula *panem et circenses*. In more recent times, even Nietzsche urged that the masses be guaranteed the maximum well-being, so that their complaints and demonstrations would not disturb the loftier manifestations of the spirit. It was an aristocratic point of view that presupposed order and prosperity—two conditions which are now a matter of chance. On the other hand, what did the Weimar republic offer the German unemployed? The spectacle of the political parties wrangling with one another and the distinguished honor of sharing, in the abstract, in popular sovereignty. As for the communists, nothing seems to me more enlightening than a confidence which the German communist Clara Zetkin records in one of her books as having been made to her by Lenin. Asked if the Bolshevik revolution hadn't been greatly helped by the fact that most Russian peasants were illiterate, Lenin answered yes, undoubtedly. Compared to all these forms of derision and deceit, Hitler seems to me on a slightly higher level when he says he wants to give the masses a new faith.

THOMAS THE CYNIC

It would be more correct to say an ersatz faith: the myth of blood and earth.

PROFESSOR PICKUP

The new faith has been accepted by the German people. Isn't that good enough for you? Isn't that a democratic criterion? No longer *panem et circenses,* therefore, but *panem et fidem.* But if faith is enough for the masses, I agree that, for the leaders, knowledge and awareness are also required. This task, it seems to me, has now been made much easier for us. Fascism's achievements in Europe are so grandiose that they offer abundant material for its scientific justification. The superiority of corporativism, for example, as a system for the organization production, can be scientifically demonstrated. Why shouldn't we extract a scientific system from its achievements and use it as our program? Why shouldn't we bring that program into public discussions—to be attended, not by the masses but by the intelligent part of the population—and prove that it corresponds to the dictates of both reason and experience?

THOMAS THE CYNIC

Do you really have such a program? I'm beginning to grow worried.

MR. DOUBLE YOU

Yes. Why keep it a secret? It was drawn up by a committee of college professors, with Professor Pickup as chairman. It's a long program. To tell you the truth, I haven't yet read it all the way through.

THOMAS THE CYNIC

I advise you to file it away and forget about it.

MR. DOUBLE YOU

The committee of professors cost me a small fortune. The program is there now, all paid for. Why shouldn't I have it printed?

THOMAS THE CYNIC

Enter the expense under the heading "charity" and forget that program. It's the only way of cutting your losses. Discuss it? Persuade people? That would be madness. An aspiring dictator must never appeal to the critical spirit of his listeners. He would be the first victim. A fascist leader must carry away, inflame, arouse his listeners, inspiring contempt and hatred for those timeservers who engage in discussions. "Talk doesn't fill your belly"—there's an effective slogan against the traditional politicians. Whatever the fascist leader says must be said as if it were self-evident, so as not to leave room for the slightest doubt or argument. Expressions such as "perhaps," "It may be that," "It seems to me," "Unless I am mistaken," must all be strictly avoided. Any invitation to discuss must be rejected. "We don't discuss the safety of the Fatherland," "We don't argue with traitors," "The unemployed want jobs, nor words"—these are answers that every follower will approve. Any other kind of behavior would be disastrous. I'll give you an example from this little country's recent history. A few years ago, as a repercussion of the fascist victories in Italy and Germany, an embryonic fascist movement called the Frontists arose in Switzerland, too. It quickly ran its course, however, after a clamorous beginning. Its failure was due in the first place to this country's lack of the peculiar political and social conditions which are the requisite of every burgeoning totalitarian movement, whether of the right or the left. But the failure of Swiss Fascism was hastened by the fact that its leaders thought to propagate fascism by agreeing to public debates with their socialist, democratic, liberal and even Jewish opponents. The results were catastrophic. I must add, however, that the poor wretches probably had no choice. Given the democratic climate of this country, if a political leader refuses a debate with his opponents, he runs the risk of disqualifying himself and not finding any supporters. And what makes things even more risky for totalitarians in Switzerland is the people's dislike of eloquence.

MR. DOUBLE YOU

Yes indeed, I've heard that the majority of politicians here aren't lawyers, as in other democracies, but schoolteachers.

THOMAS THE CYNIC

Yes, in this respect Switzerland has remained the country of Pestalozzi. But, luckily for fascism, not all democratic countries resemble Switzerland. In most of them if eloquence were banned, what would be left of democracy?

In these attempts to smuggle fascism into Switzerland, there were quite a few young scholars who, like Professor Pickup, tried to extract a theory of fascism from an analysis of the recently introduced state institutions of Italy and Germany. It's a typical intellectual's error. There's a saying that intellectuality and intelligence often have nothing in common, and it's true that intellectuals are easily attracted by the formal and narrowly juridical side of social reality. It's the fault of this kind of intellectual that democracy has become a synonym of parliamentarianism, and Bolshevism, a synonym of Soviet, even where parliamentarianism has destroyed democracy and even after Bolshevism had eliminated the Soviets. As far as fascism is concerned, Mr. Double You, keep this in mind: it must not be considered identical with any of the expressions it has hitherto assumed, with any of the institutions it has created since achieving power. Fascism is always nationalistic, but not obligatorily anti-Semitic; it always creates mass organizations, but not necessarily corporations. Its institutions are simulacra which fulfill secondary functions, and only law professors can take them seriously.

PROFESSOR PICKUP

It's been a long time since I witnessed such a distortion of the truth. If I wanted to, Mr. Cynic, I could overwhelm you with quotations to prove that Mussolini didn't disdain arguments and programs.

THOMAS THE CYNIC

I don't doubt it, so you can spare yourself the trouble. Mussolini unquestionably had a vocation for power, but he was a bit slow to discover the rules of the totalitarian game. The reform programs you're

referring to didn't facilitate his victory; they complicated it. You can find the most contradictory concepts in his writings, even on the fundamental question of the State. In April 1920 he allowed himself to
write: "Down with the State in all its forms and in
whatever incarnation. The state of yesterday, today,
tomorrow, the bourgeois state and the socialist state.
To us, the last survivors of individualism, there is
nothing left, to get us through the present night and
that of tomorrow, save the now absurd but always
consoling religion of Anarchy." Those were Mussolini's own words.

MR. DOUBLE YOU
    As late as the spring of 1920?

THOMAS THE CYNIC
    In August 1922, however, he wrote: "The cen-
tury of democracy is finished. An aristocratic century, our own, succeeds the last. The State that belongs to all will end up by becoming once again the
State of the few. The new generations forbid that
democracy's bulky corpse shall block the pathways
to the future." Finally, after seizing power, he took
yet another turn. "For Fascism," he wrote, "the State
is the absolute, compared to which individuals and
groups are only the relative." The rapid parabola had
ended. After which, nobody should try to ascribe
Mussolini's success to the clarity of his ideas on the
question of the State.

PROFESSOR PICKUP
    Despite Mussolini's avowedly absolutist am-
bitions, the present Italian government is in many

ways less totalitarian than the German. Undoubtedly Hitler had a more coherent vision of his goal. "The state is a means toward an end," he wrote, "and the end is the preservation of the race."

THOMAS THE CYNIC

But Mussolini didn't lack the talent of piling emphasis on the most hackneyed formulas. "We are against renunciations, we are for our rights," he used to say. "We are against irresponsibility, we are for the respect of values," he often repeated. Mind that word "values." You can make unlimited use of it; it sounds well, and it doesn't commit you to anything.

MR. DOUBLE YOU

By the way, what does *eia eia alalà* mean?

THOMAS THE CYNIC

Nothing. It was a cry D'Annunzio invented during the war. You will find no trace of it in any language or dialect, and its own inventor gave it no rational meaning. Therefore it had all the prerequisites for becoming one of the responses of the Fascist ritual. When that response is shouted by an excited crowd, it assumes a meaning laden with emotion and can express, according to the circumstances, amazement, ecstasy, pleading, begging, eagerness for sacrifice. For the success of a fascist movement, such words are more valuable than any theoretical treatise on corporations. The very fact that it is formed almost always of inarticulate sounds is a somewhat startling throwback to what must have been the cries of the cave men. *Alalà, a noi, heil* are the liturgical formulas which open and close every Fascist or Nazi manifestation. The psalm-like chanting of incomprehensible texts has been a precious resource of mass religions in every age. Latin has never kept illiterate peasants from attending Catholic rites; on the contrary, it has always been a big help in attracting them.

PROFESSOR PICKUP

Marx's *Das Kapital*, too. If it had been written in a more comprehensible style, it would have been less popular.

THOMAS THE CYNIC

No party has ever failed to exploit this human weakness, but fascism has built its entire fortune on it, creating the modern technique of political hypnotic suggestion. You can't deny fascism that merit at least.

MR. DOUBLE YOU

In Berlin we met a certain Dr. Guterer, the Grand Master of Ceremonies for National Socialism's public manifestations. Speaking with him, I realized why German churches and theatres are so empty nowadays; both liturgy and play acting have moved into the public squares.

THOMAS THE CYNIC

In the squares you can also see the symbols and fetishes of the new idolatry: the eagles, swastikas, fasces, flags. Napoleon said once, "Give me a button and I will make people live or die for it." Napoleon's experiment was a success. Every Fascist and Nazi wears the party emblem in his buttonhole and proclaims himself willing to give his life for it. That button guarantees its bearer the protection of its sacred power; it serves to distinguish the fascist from other men and establish his superiority over the poor wretches who don't have one. The newspapers tell how some fascists kiss the button when they are dying; others insist on being buried with it, as an amulet against the powers of hell; others place it for a moment on the forehead of their newborn son so that he may grow up dedicated to the Fatherland. The flag of the neighborhood club ceases to be a stick and a piece of cloth the moment that the Leader's representative touches it. The new provincial offices are no longer just one more building after the Leader's representative has opened the door. The symbol ends by being confused with the thing it represents. The flag doesn't stand for the country; it *is* the country. Any attempt to explain the efficacy of a fetish by its form or color would be arbitrary. The power of a fetish lies solely in the mind of its worshipers: the German National Socialist flag is large and red, whereas that of the Italian Fascist party is small and black, and yet they fulfill the same function and with the same results.

PROFESSOR PICKUP

Why did the symbols of dictatorship prove more powerful than those of its opponents? Ha ha. Explain that one to me.

THOMAS THE CYNIC

Whenever a democratic or socialist party uses a symbol, it is accompanied by an ideology that prevents—or at least discourages—its being turned into a fetish. For the worker, socialism is something concrete—wages, factory, home. In that case, the flag remains simply a flag. The same can be said of oratory. The leader of a totalitarian movement usually isn't a great orator in the traditional sense. At times he recalls the war propagandists who harangued the troops before battle and at other times exactly the opposite—the improvised leader of mutinied soldiers. And yet that violent, coarse way of speaking only draws the masses closer to him, and they end by feeling that it is their own voice they hear. That is the style of fascist eloquence—false and artificial like all other styles of eloquence but, for the masses who have known the war and long unemployment, infinitely more effective than the old "operatic" eloquence of Gambetta, Jaurès, Lassalle, Enrico Ferri, Lloyd George. It's the superiority of Al Jolson over Caruso.

MR. DOUBLE YOU

Have you ever heard of Van Buren? In 1828 he helped Jackson to the presidency with an overwhelming election campaign whose slogan was the defense of the "people's sacred rights." Nobody was threatening those rights, least of all John Quincy Adams, the outgoing President, but Van Buren's slogan had a wild success. Van Buren himself succeeded Jackson as president, and he was forced to witness the efficacy of his miraculous recipe when, standing for re-election, he found himself opposed by Harrison, presented as "the man of the people," and the "log-cabin man," the simple, modest, sober family man as opposed to Van Buren who, being President, lived in a palace with a whole lot of servants and ate with gold knives and forks.

THOMAS THE CYNIC

Forgive me, I am truly mortified. You Americans have nothing to learn from a European.

9.

*How democracy devours itself, with a
few useful examples of the art of
fishing in troubled waters.*

PROFESSOR PICKUP

Any onlooker at fascist public meetings must admit that the masses participate as actively as in those of other parties. Even more so. . . .

THOMAS THE CYNIC

And from that you would infer that fascism is democratic?

PROFESSOR PICKUP

In the good sense of the word, of course. Since the word democracy comes from *demos*.

THOMAS THE CYNIC

So, according to you, the guerrilla fighting of the Chouans and Vendée peasants against the Convention was a democratic movement?

PROFESSOR PICKUP

Historians say it wasn't, because those peasants were under the political guidance of the clergy and nobility. But you surely can't deny that most fascist leaders are of humble origin and were granted power by universal suffrage.

THOMAS THE CYNIC

Many, many violations of freedom have been

sanctioned by universal suffrage. In his essay "La revolution sociale démontrée par le coup d'état du 2
decembre," written towards the middle of the last
century, Proudhon asked himself: "Who elected the
Constituent Assembly, filled with legitimists, monar-
chists, nobles, generals and prelates? Universal
suffrage. Who ratified the coup of the 2nd of December? Universal suffrage." And so on. Those questions,
which refer to a few years of French political history,
could be followed up by similar questions today, hundreds of them.

MR. DOUBLE YOU

To be blunt then, Mr. Cynic, if democracy isn't
universal suffrage, what is it, according to you?

THOMAS THE CYNIC

It's only in recent times that democracy has come
to have the generic meaning of government by the
majority of the people. Until 1848 it meant political
power supported by the poor part of the nation, the
peasants, artisans, workers and the *petite bourgeoisie*.
Universal suffrage was then considered an instrument
of democracy, not its essence. Events have proved that
extending the vote does not always result in a strength-
ening of democracy. And examples are not lacking
of cases where the reactionaries extended the vote
with the specific purpose of weakening democracy.
Mere numbers without minds of their own are so
much ballast which can be put to any use.

PROFESSOR PICKUP

That reminds me of a talk we had with Guglielmo

Ferrero, whom we visited in Geneva. The democratic reforms introduced in Italy after 1880 by King Umberto had manifestly reactionary intentions, Ferrero told us. The number of electors was increased from one hundred and fifty thousand to two million. The king thought that an electorate of two million people, mostly poor and ignorant, could be manipulated by government better than an electorate of one hundred and fifty thousand people. And in point of fact he was right. Under the appearance of a broader democracy, King Umberto was able to strengthen the independence of the executive.

THOMAS THE CYNIC

In the Italian communes of the Middle Ages, the *Signorie* did the same thing, winning support from the humble people against the eminent families. In the same way royal absolutism used the middle classes to resist the nobility. Peter the Great defeated the nationalist movement of Mazeppa in the Ukraine by granting some of the poor people's claims and by dividing the Cossacks from their leader. But fascism has the distinction of having perfected the art of modern democracy with the instruments that democracy itself had forged.

MR. DOUBLE YOU

You're not trying to say that the operation is lawful only when carried out by a party with a traditional name, are you?

THOMAS THE CYNIC

I'm not trying to say anything. Only to clarify ideas.

MR. DOUBLE YOU
I'm listening to you.

THOMAS THE CYNIC
In modern times the death of a democracy is, more often than not, camouflaged suicide. A regime of freedom should receive its lifeblood from the self-government of local institutions. When democracy, driven by some of its baser tendencies, suppresses such autonomies, it is only devouring itself. If in the factory the master's word is law, if bureaucracy takes over the trade union, if the central government's representative runs the city and the province, and the leader's henchman controls the local branches of political parties, then you can no longer speak of democracy. Unfortunately, the democratic and socialist parties have always been, at least in Europe, the most active in promoting centralization to the detriment of local and regional autonomy, following the tradition of the Jacobins, who felt that the hegemony of the capital over the rest of the country provided them with a weapon in the struggle against the priests and the nobles. Another cause of the centralization of democratic and socialist parties can be found in the fact that their adherents, peasants, workers and lower middle class, are among the poorest of the population, and it seems necessary for the national government to assist them. In this way the All-Providing State is born. While the constant subsidies and protective laws of the state increase the supporters of the socialist and democratic parties, at the same time they stifle local autonomy. So in the history of some countries you can observe this apparent contradiction: the maximum material and numerical strength of the democratic and

socialist parties immediately precedes the collapse of democracy.

PROFESSOR PICKUP

About a hundred years ago De Tocqueville wrote that if freedom is one day suppressed in America, it will be because of the tyranny of the majority, who will finally drive the minorities to defend their existence by unconstitutional means. Many symptoms of that democratic tyranny can already be seen in our country, and it's quite clear that the future fortunes of American Fascism depend on the illegal reaction of discontented minorities.

MR. DOUBLE YOU

Those old terms "majority" and "minority" once stood for conflicts of opinion, but they don't have the same meaning any more, and I think they should be replaced with the term "party apparatuses" or "machines."

THOMAS THE CYNIC

At all events, that's one up for the totalitarians. An Italo-German sociologist, Roberto Michels, has demonstrated that the internal life of every mass party tends towards oligarchy. Lip service is paid to the members' sovereignty at party congresses, but these are actually manipulated by the small group of bosses. In the plenary sessions, the provincial delegates are allowed to applaud or boo the great party orators, while the important decisions are arranged at small committee meetings. The closing session is reserved for the election of the new executive committee; this election is usually held at a late hour in the evening, when many of the delegates are already at the station. Amid general lack of attention, a show of hands is called, by which the congress again delegates its sovereign power to the dominant oligarchy. If there are any exceptions to this rule, they are to be found only at congresses in backward countries, or at those of small parties with no hope of gaining power.

MR. DOUBLE YOU

That isn't the case with our two great parties, thank God. If you're never been to one, you can't imagine what our national conventions are like, when they choose the presidential candidate every four years. You can have a faint notion if you take a circus on a Sunday evening, add a county fair, and on top of that, the infernal racket of a stock market on a day when stocks are falling. Add also the frenzied lights and sounds of a masked ball. At the concluding session the spectacle reaches terrifying heights; everyone shouts, sings, waves noisemakers, whistles, and a number of bands all play at once. Meanwhile, in a quiet hotel room four or five people are bargaining and deciding.

THOMAS THE CYNIC

You can continue to pile it on; I won't contradict you. But, with the sole aim of clarifying ideas and without trying to convert you, I would like you to realize that fascism—like any other totalitarian movement—doesn't arise to correct the faults of democracy, but to magnify them to the point of paroxysm and destroy any residual good qualities.

MR. DOUBLE YOU

What good qualities?

THOMAS THE CYNIC

Those that mass civilization, centralization and bureaucratization haven't yet managed to eradicate completely: the plurality of political parties, freedom of the press, freedom of education, religious freedom, an independent workers' organization. . . .

MR. DOUBLE YOU

You can stop reeling off your list, since it would be impossible to examine, one by one, these self-styled good qualities of democracy. But, just to make concepts clear, as we have agreed, I'm particularly interested in getting to the bottom of the question of workers' organizations. I admit that the impressions I gathered in Italy and Germany on that score are confused and contradictory.

THOMAS THE CYNIC

In all European countries, up to the time of fascism, workers' organizations and socialism coincided and often were confused, both as concepts and as a force, even though in some countries the Catholics had succeeded in creating their own trade union movement. And since workers' organizations are now considered an indispensable element in regulating the labor market, it seemed that socialism was invincible and irreplaceable, in the interest of the economy itself. Fascism gave socialism a hard blow by proving that the organization of the great working masses could be used for antisocial ends. When fascism showed that socialism could be separated from the workers' organizations, it damaged socialism more than when it killed the Marxist leaders and closed down their premises. The German experience has confirmed the Italian lesson. From it one may conclude that a reorganization of the working class along totalitarian lines is an inescapable necessity for the totalitarian state.

PROFESSOR PICKUP

The masses, Goebbels has written, are a weak, lazy, cowardly agglomeration of men. The masses are amorphous material. Only through the achievement of a statesman can the masses become a people and the people a nation.

THOMAS THE CYNIC

Winning over the working classes, however, isn't within everyone's ability. Probably every antisocial attempt likely to be undertaken in the countries which are still democratic will wear a popular, even a plebeian, disguise and will try to make progress among the workers by alternating the methods of violence with those of demagogy, creating its own unions or seizing the already existing ones. The most suitable leader for such an undertaking must not only have the personal qualities we've already mentioned, but must also come from a humble background and know the working class well. It would be a good thing if he's worked for the socialist party, or even better if he has been a communist. In France (a country with a great tradition along this line) they say that ex-poachers make the best gamekeepers.

PROFESSOR PICKUP

Precisely. The necessity to win over the workers inspired Hitler in choosing the name of his party.

The name of the movement, he wrote, must from the very beginning offer the widest possible appeal to the masses.

THOMAS THE CYNIC

Mussolini, too, though he was expelled from the Socialist Party in 1914 for being an interventionist, continued to give his newspaper *Il Popolo d'Italia* the subtitle "A Socialist Daily." Later he replaced this with "The Producers' Daily." In September 1921, when the question of changing Fascism from a movement into a party was being discussed, Mussolini first thought of calling it the Fascist Labor Party. The word "labor" he said, is indispensable to the name of a new party. In 1919 he entertained the hope of separating the workers' unions from the Socialist party and, with the help of their right wing, creating a true Italian labor party, following the English model. But that plan failed because the militant workers recalled his 1914 "betrayal" and refused to have anything to do with him, considering him an "untouchable." So he was forced to go his own way. For a while he advocated the system of a single trade union, but he ended up by creating separate Fascist unions. At the first congress of these Fascist unions, Mussolini explained himself by saying in effect: If you want to live, you must sabotage and destroy the enemy, in all his hiding places, in all his trenches; Fascism has formed a trade union as a physiological necessity of its development.

MR. DOUBLE YOU

I've heard it said that the struggle between fascism and socialism in Europe was a civil war within the socialist movement. I gather that whoever said it wasn't entirely wrong.

THOMAS THE CYNIC

A single principle seems to have guided Mussolini and Hitler every time they had the choice of taking part, by whatever means, in the struggle of workers against entrepreneurs: incite to disorder, aggravate disorder, maintain disorder as an endemic condition. For only prolonged disorder can justify the installation of a dictatorship. Systematic disorder paralyzes social and economic life, makes foreign relations difficult, increases poverty, throws irremediable discredit on established institutions, renders all plans uncertain, and finally makes dictatorship seem the only hope of salvation. Permanent disorder creates the spiritual conditions in which the man in the street loses his patience, abandons all self-control, and keeps repeating to everyone he meets, even strangers: "I don't care who comes next, even if it's the devil himself, just so long as he governs the country properly and puts an end to this chaos once and for all." Disorder is for fascism what humus is for a plant. In the Goebbels diary of the Berlin transport strike of November 1932, where Nazis and Communists fought amicably together to make the strike succeed, there are some very revealing pages on this subject. Goebbels records with irony the shocked comments of the democratic press at that apparently unnatural alliance, and he notes in lyrical terms the acts of violence that the strikers committed against the Social-Democrat scabs. "Our party apparatus," he writes proudly, "works splendidly. In every clash our men are leading the violence. There are already four dead and countless wounded, both among workers and police. The authorities say that the financial conditions of the transport company make it impossible to grant the workers' requests. These considerations," Goebbels remarks, "are no concern of ours. An opposition has a right to ask even what the government cannot give."

PROFESSOR PICKUP

You've fallen into a flagrant contradiction. On other occasions, as I well remember, you told us that fascism developed in Germany and Italy with the support of the landowners and the industrialists; now on the contrary you're trying to convince us that fascism and Nazism were so anxious to win over the masses and increase disorder that they actually encouraged and organized strikes, either in alliance or in competition with the Marxists. Don't you see that the two attitudes are incompatible?

THOMAS THE CYNIC

Only in appearance. If you give me your attention for a moment, the example of Italian Fascism will serve to clarify the bond between these two attitudes which you find incompatible. In the first place, you must remember that capitalism isn't a homogeneous thing. Fascist demagogy continued for a long time to be directed against two particular categories of property owners—merchants and landlords of urban property—without arousing the displeasure of other capitalists. Towards the end of June and the beginning of July 1919, there were popular uprisings against retail merchants in many Italian cities. Many shops were wrecked, goods were distributed free, or else confiscated and sold at a discount of fifty per cent. In var-

ious cities the fomenters of this movement were, in
fact, the Fascists, assisted by gangs of veterans. Mussolini openly encouraged this action. "I demand a fir-
ing squad for shopkeepers who starve the people," he
wrote in his newspaper in mid-June, a few days before the riots. As soon as the destruction of the shops
began, he expressed his approval. "Revolt is absolutely
necessary to strike down these leeches," he wrote. "In
Bergamo they have started hunting down the exploit-
ers, and we cannot but approve. In Romagna the
people are rebelling violently against the corruption
of the speculators. It wasn't the Socialist party that un-
leashed and directed these demonstrations. We approve the fundamental justice of these protests of the
people."

MR. DOUBLE YOU

Were most of those shopkeepers Jews?

THOMAS THE CYNIC

No. Nature and history have rained many afflic-
tions on my country, but we have been spared one at
least: Italians don't know the meaning of anti-Semi-
tism. The percentage of Jews in the Italian population
is very slight and is perhaps more noticeable among
wholesalers than among retail merchants. Now, as I
have said, the victims of those riots were exclusively
shopkeepers. It would be hard to imagine a more stupid and demagogical campaign against the high cost of
living. Another category of capitalists against which
the Fascists enjoyed staging cheap demonstrations at
that time was, as I have said, that of the landlords. And
finally, state-operated businesses. In Italy, in addition
to various monopolies like those of salt and tobacco,

the State operates the railroads and the postal, telegraph and telephone systems. Fascist agitation among the public utility workers didn't displease private capitalists, who had never looked favorably on the State's assuming gainful economic occupations. After the seizure of power, not only did Fascism suppress the public servant's right to strike, but even his right to form a union. In the period when Fascism was in opposition, however, it approved and supported them, beginning with the first economic agitation of railroad and postal workers at the end of 1919. Moreover, as long as Mussolini believed in the possibility of a proletarian revolution, his attitude towards private industrialists was circumspect. He differed from the socialists at that time mainly on the question of how best to exploit Italy's military victory; on all other questions he was an eclectic. In September 1921, when the workers occupied the factories, Mussolini sent an expression of solidarity to the leaders of the movement. It might have been the beginning of the proletarian revolution and it was best not to miss the bus. But the movement came to a bad end. Then Fascism tried to make sure that the defeat of the proletarian extremists and the simultaneous improvement in the country's economy didn't restore the country to a feeling of security. That would have been the end. Fascism promoted a civil war against the working class, which was now on the defensive. To show you what that bloody struggle was like, I need only to quote a single sentence from the *Memoirs of a Fascist*, written by one Umberto Bianchelli of Florence. "For quite some time," he wrote, "anyone who happened to have a working class appearance was liable, as he walked down the street, to be assaulted without mercy by a Fascist squad." Toward the end of 1921 the Florentine industrialists, thinking that the communist menace was over, decided that it was no longer necessary to finance these squads for the beating up of workers; whereupon the Fascists expressed their surprise and indignation in a public manifesto, warning that "faced with the hostility of the rich and the idle bourgeoisie, which applauds Fascist action as long as it coincides with their material interests, the Fascists formally declare that starting today they withdraw from the struggle." Everyone took this announcement as explicitly inviting the communists to resume and intensify their action, so that the rich, no longer defended by the Fascists, would tremble with fear and be forced to resume their financial support. Similar manifestos appeared at that time in other cities too, thanks to the local *Fasci*, which were infuriated at the thought of being dismissed as useless or because the country wanted to live in peace. They had no difficulty in provoking incidents to show that, on the contrary, the Fascists were more indispensable than ever.

MR. DOUBLE YOU

Nothing is more natural than that an unemployed fireman should turn to arson.

THOMAS THE CYNIC

There was no shortage of inflammable material. Even though, between the spring of 1920 and that of 1922, Fascism had destroyed all the peasant leagues and socialist cooperatives of the Po Valley, it didn't risk dying of idleness, since the great mass of agricultural day-laborers, forced into the Fascist trade-unions, was still agitated because of unemployment. Only one thing was changed: while the socialists had always managed to direct that malcontent against the land-owners, the Fascists turned it against the State. Among other things, there was a memorable March on Bologna in April 1922, in which forty-five thousand unemployed of that province were led by the Fascist Italo Balbo. So, despite the ties that linked Fascism to the propertied classes and the state apparatus, Fascism set no limit to its instigation of disorder in the country, arousing the resentment of each class against another, and that of all classes against democratic institutions.

MR. DOUBLE YOU

I think there's an English expression for that: "Fishing in troubled waters."

THOMAS THE CYNIC

We have the same expression in Italy. In other words, before it seizes power, Fascism must be a net designed especially for fishing in troubled waters. With its subversive appearance, it can easily play the role of heir to socialism, usurping the place of the old idol in the imagination of the masses. In Germany this happened on a wider scale and more easily than in Italy.

PROFESSOR PICKUP

In New York we discussed this subject with the psychologist Erich Fromm. It isn't hard to switch the aim of a revolution, he said, provided its structure remains unaltered.

THOMAS THE CYNIC

Sometimes the continuity of that structure is contained in a single word. I'll just tell you one episode to explain what I mean. In August 1922 the Alleanza del Lavoro, a cartel of Italian antifascist unions and parties, declared a nationwide general strike. A group of Fascist post-office employees, ex-socialists, met in Rome to discuss what was to be done. The orders of the Fascist Party were to sabotage the strike. But sabotaging a strike meant scorn, hatred, dirty names from their fellow workers. It would mean betraying their class. So these neo-Fascists were considerably embarrassed. But while the meeting was in progress, another order of Mussolini's arrived from Milan. It didn't say anything new, but it contained the word that rescued them. The magic sentence was this: "The antifascists who are on strike are not true revolutionaries; *we* are the true revolutionaries." All present instantly sighed with relief. They looked at one another, smiling and reassured: "Aha, we're the true revolutionaries after all; and if we don't go out and stand by our fellow workers, it's only because they're not true revolutionaries." One of the protagonists of this episode subsequently published an account of it.

PROFESSOR PICKUP

I'm reminded of a statement Hitler made in a Munich courtroom : "If I stand here today as a revolutionary, it's as a revolutionary against the revolution." And this also explains many of his superficial, openly plebeian concessions to the taste of his opponents. But it doesn't explain everything.

MR. DOUBLE YOU

If the Fascists had adopted top hats and tails, instead of the black or brown shirt, I imagine that their appeal to the workers would have been considerably less.

It isn't the first time that a political movement has been defined by some sartorial peculiarity of its members. The peasant revolts around Beauvais in the middle of the twelfth century were called the *jacquerie* because of the *jacque*, the jacket, which then distinguished the peasants from the nobles and priests. A few centuries later the followers of the Jacobins were called *sans-culottes* because instead of the aristocratic knee-length *culottes* they work long trousers, in the bourgeois fashion that we still follow today. Toward the second half of the last century, in Sweden under Gustav III, there were two parties in violent opposition: the caps and the hats. The caps were for Russia, and the hats for France.

In the cases you mention, my dear professor, and in others that could be added, the article of clothing that gave its name to the movement was actually worn in everyday life by the people taking part. The origin of the black or brown shirt is very different. Before Fascism, the black shirt in Italy was normal wear for certain categories of workers when on the job, not for esthetic reasons, needless to say, but for the sake of economy, since black doesn't show the dirt. Neither Mussolini nor those of his supporters who helped him found the first *Fasci* had ever worn a black shirt for reasons of economy; and even later, when the *Fasci* became larger and more numerous, the workers were always a minority. So the choice of the black shirt as the party uniform was meant to disguise the social origins of the movement. It gave the movement a superficially plebeian and rebellious character, even when it was worn on armed expeditions against Socialist party offices by students, officers, shopkeepers' sons and rich farmers.

PROFESSOR PICKUP

You must avoid generalizing from the Italian experience, Mr. Cynic. There have been other fascist movements which proclaimed themselves, from the first, to be uncompromisingly aristocratic. Take the Rumanian movement founded in 1924 by Godreanu. It was christened "The Archangel Michael" to express its idealistic and mystic aspirations. Or take the Rexists in Belgium or the *Croix du Feu* in France.

MR. DOUBLE YOU

These movements you're talking about—did they ever get into power?

PROFESSOR PICKUP

No, on the contrary . . .

MR. DOUBLE YOU

In that case, let's skip them. We're talking about politics, not poetry. The impression I got from my German trip, Mr. Cynic, doesn't coincide altogether with what you say. I didn't think the anticapitalism of the Nazis was merely tactical or for show. I saw a real leveling of the classes, obviously brought about by the new spirit in politics and in the army. We've achieved the same thing in America. Thanks to our prosperity you can't tell a worker's son from a banker's, at least not at first sight.

THOMAS THE CYNIC

There's something in what you say, but it's really difficult to express a final estimate of Nazism's social policy, which so far has followed a zig-zag course. In 1919-20, Germany's capitalist economy was in such bad shape that nobody, not even the capitalists, dared defend it. The only question discussed was what measures should be taken to bring about a new economic regime. Among the aims of National Socialism which Hitler announced to the public at the end of February 1920, a certain number were decidedly anticapitalistic: nationalization of the trusts, municipalization of the great department stores, participation by the workers in the profits of the big factories, confiscation of all war profits, expropriation without indemnity of land required for public use, abolition of income from land, death sentence against usurers and speculators. These aims were popular, shared also by other parties, and in line with the desires of the great majority of Germans.

If, despite all the talk and planning of a new economy, nothing was achieved, German capitalists should be particularly grateful to the Social Democrats. Hitler made the first correction to his platform in August of that same year, declaring that industrial capital should be respected and that the struggle should aim only at Jewish capital employed in speculation. As to the question of confiscating land for public use, the Nazi Rosenberg still insisted, at the beginning of 1923, that there be no compensation, but he restricted the government's right of confiscation to lands needed for building roads and canals. The party's political development and its relationship with the industrialists led finally to a revision of the rest of the platform. In 1928 Hitler explained that the only lands to be confiscated were those whose purchase could be proved illegal and which were not cultivated according to the general interest. He further explained that this move was directed "primarily against Jewish companies engaged in land speculation." In his tract "Das Programm der NSDAP," Feder had observed that a proper concept of labor will inevitably foster respect for private property. The same author, in his "Kampf gegen die Hochfinanz," had made a distinction which was not devoid of humor; "We do not reject," he wrote, "the collaboration of honest bankers." There have naturally been some, such as Otto Strasser, who took a different view; but Hitler, in arguing with him, went so far as to say that for Nazism the social structure couldn't be a matter of principle, since all the masses want is to eat well and enjoy themselves.

MR. DOUBLE YOU

To my mind, that opinion can't be refuted.

THOMAS THE CYNIC

At all events, Otto Strasser and Goebbels were allowed, because of the necessity to penetrate the milieu of the communist-influenced workers, to go on talking of socialization, even when it had long been shelved as a real objective of National Socialism. The first step toward liquidating the generic anticapitalism of their early days was disguised by the distinction between "parasitical capitalism and productive capitalism." Healthy, productive capitalism was not to be condemned, only some of its degenerations which had sprung up like poisonous mushrooms out of the war and the inflation. A second step was achieved by superimposing the images of socialism and of nation and confusing (but this often happens outside Germany too) "socialism" with "social." This doesn't alter the fact the Germany's present rearmament, while fattening certain capitalist groups, is costing others painful sacrifices. In Italy there have been the same developments, but on a less dramatic scale. The crisis of capitalism was not as serious as in Germany, nor the Italian proletariat as tough. That's why Mussolini was able to pass easily from his socialist-tinged aims to his apologia of capitalism, and finally to the empty verbalism of so-called corporativism.

MR. DOUBLE YOU

I know there are fifty-two different ways of cooking a couple of eggs. Before coming to Europe, I had a talk with the Archbishop of Cincinnati, Monsignor McNicholas. That reverend prelate said to me, in so many words: As far as economic regimes are concerned, Catholicism is agnostic. It was born in ancient times, in countries whose economy was based on slaves; it prospered in the Middle Ages with feudalism, it adapted itself to capitalism, and it will be perfectly capable of adapting itself to socialism.

Those words are sacrosanct, especially for a politician. The important thing is power. Whether you rule over slaves or serfs or workers or bourgeois or bankers is a secondary matter. The important thing is to rule. I accept whatever economic regime I find. If I were a Soviet citizen, naturally I'd try to achieve power by respecting collective property and adorning my speeches with quotations from Lenin. Being an American citizen, I behave with coherence and I try to find the right path to the achievement of my purpose.

10.

*The art of double-dealing and the
danger of believing in one's
own deceptions.*

MR. DOUBLE YOU

For me, the only advantage of insomnia is the opportunity to ponder what has been said and done during the day, Now, last night I began to suspect that in our recent meetings we've been talking about the internal situation of the United States too superficially. In reality, things are very complicated. People back home, for example—the least stupid ones anyway—are beginning to get bored and fed-up with all that moronic sales talk in the advertisements.

THOMAS THE CYNIC

In that case all you have to do is invent new slogans along the lines of "Down with Slogans." When a sick man can't bear to hear medicines mentioned, a clever doctor continues to prescribe them, but is careful to call them antimedicines.

THOMAS THE CYNIC

If this tendency should continue, you would be wise to adopt "Down with fascism" as your motto. Mind you, it wouldn't be anything new. In 1926 Pilsudski forced his dictatorship on Poland with the cry "Down with dictatorship." For that matter, did any tyrant ever take over a nation without waving the flag of "true freedom"?

PROFESSOR PICKUP

I don't feel like arguing about your peculiar reminiscences, but I must express my disgust at your line of reasoning. Are you really serious? How is one to recognize a fascist if he fights his way to power with the phraseology of the democratic party? How is anyone to understand politics if each side gets into the habit of saying the opposite of what it thinks, if the internationalist begins to defend nationalism and the nationalist starts talking about world brotherhood, or the communist rants about peace among the classes and the Christian foments civil wars? At this rate we'll end up rebuilding the Tower of Babel.

THOMAS THE CYNIC

That has already been done, my dear Professor, at least as far as politics is concerned. Just take a look at the newspapers, at the posters on the walls, or listen to a few political speeches. A party that springs up to fight socialism and defend the interests of property owners will be sure to disguise itself with the name "social" or "popular" or even "socialist." If a party calls itself "radical," it's bound to be moderate. If a splinter group leaves an old party to form a new one, it will inevitably call itself, not the "secessionist," but the "united" party. And if a party receives funds and orders from abroad, you may be sure it will talk constantly of national independence. Thanks to this political nomenclature, newspapers now are often filled with a macabre irony. When troops are sent to fan a civil war in a friendly country, this is called, as you know, non-intervention. When political opponents are arrested, sometimes to be shot later "while attempting escape," this is called *Schutzhaft*, or "preventive arrest." Party tribunals set up to terrorize public opinion are known as "people's courts." Armament is everywhere justified as a peace measure; promises are broken on the pretext that honor must be defended; Italy enslaves Abyssinia in order to suppress slavery; Japan invades China to free the Chinese people from the dictatorship of the Kuomintang. Lying has become so habitual that it's downright boring. It's not surprising that in these conditions totalitarian parties should feel obliged to carry mystification to extremes.

PROFESSOR PICKUP

We discussed this before, and you didn't convince me. I think it would be pointless to go over the subject again.

MR. DOUBLE YOU

But, Mr. Cynic, you surely don't mean to make lying a rule?

THOMAS THE CYNIC

No, no, the only rule for the aspiring dictator is the desire for power. The rest, whether truth or lies, must simply follow his best interests. But I don't have to teach you these things, Mr. Double You. There's just one remark I'd like to make: when a man sets out to sway others, he often remains swayed himself. It sometimes happens that by dint of constantly repeating the same lie a political orator will end up by believing it himself.

MR. DOUBLE YOU

Isn't that the height of virtuosity? Surely an actor can't move his audience if he doesn't identify himself with the fiction that he is playing.

THOMAS THE CYNIC

I'm afraid I must contradict you. What you say

applies only to mediocre actors. A great actor, when he is acting, never forgets that it is all a game. Only on this condition can he pass from one mood to another at a pace which often summarizes in the space of an hour the psychological development of many years. For the politician, too, this precaution is essential. Political sincerity, like theatrical sincerity, demands inner detachment and unremitting self-control; it is not to be confused with the sincerity of the ordinary man. For an example of supreme mastery in lying, you should read Napoleon's famous speech to the Council of State. By becoming a Catholic, he said, I ended the war in the Vendée; by becoming a Moslem, I established myself in Egypt; and by becoming an Ultramontanist, I won over the priests in Italy. If I ruled a nation of Jews, he concluded, I would rebuild the temple of Solomon. And finally I would like to recall an extreme case of opportunism which is usually glossed over. Think of those queens who, by long tradition (even in poetry), are held up to the people as symbols of every virtue, especially of faithfulness. Then think of the ease with which, encouraged by the highest ecclesiastical authorities, they renounce their childhood religion and embrace another, heretical one, if reasons of state or marriage demand it.

PROFESSOR PICKUP

You don't mean to imply that queens should submit to regulations suitable, at best, for domestic servants?

THOMAS THE CYNIC

I'm not sure what you mean, Professor, but by reserving the virtue of coherence to domestic servants, you give them a dignity that sets them above queens.

In any case, we are straying from our subject. I mentioned the examples of queens and of Napoleon only to illustrate their casual attitude to what normally are matters of principle. The aspiring dictator must be prepared to imitate them. He can engage in double-dealing or tell lies in tones of apparent sincerity, but he must be careful not to be trapped by his own deceptions. Otherwise he is in danger on two counts: he loses all sense of the possible and he is liable to tilt at windmills.

MR. DOUBLE YOU

To sum up: you can tell an intelligent politician by the speed with which he sees a situation changing and takes the necessary precautions. Is that it?

THOMAS THE CYNIC

Precisely. If you look for the causes of the mistakes Mussolini and Hitler made in their rise to power, you'll find that they were all due to delay in recognizing new situations and adapting to them. The damage wasn't irreparable only because their political opponents were bound hand and foot to outdated methods and traditions. In some cases, the fascist leaders' errors consisted in affectionate attachments to the dreams and symbols of their youth (like the republicanism and anticlericalism that Mussolini couldn't shake off even when he was drawing his supporters from monarchist and clerical groups). This temptation to be coherent with his past, if it comes when fortune has already smiled at the aspiring dictator, can also indicate a dangerous streak of vanity. I'd almost call it a need for self-respect, a desire to believe himself the equal of his opponents, who talk constantly of

"world-view" and "ethical ideal" and who, the dictator feels, scorn him as a vulgar adventurer. This comprehensible temptation turned the heads of both Mussolini and Hitler for several weeks before they
achieved power. They overcame the temptation only
when they realized that their destiny was different
and that they would be lost if they tried to change it.
Success, with the self-intoxication it inspires, aggra-
vated by the fawning adulation of their followers,
can lead the future dictator to an exaggerated opinion
of himself and to the false belief that the future of
both party and country depends henceforth on his
whim alone. This might be called the delusion of the
fly on the rear wheel who thinks he is driving the
coach. If it doesn't always lead to disaster, it inevitably
causes searing humiliations.

PROFESSOR PICKUP

You have a talent for debasing everything, Mr.
Cynic. Why must you forget that the fascist leader
is the bearer of a new world view, the creator of a new
collective spirit? In that capacity, and thanks to his
identification with the great masses of the nation, he
can rise above the level of the ordinary politician—
who is tied to private interests—and he acquires the
gift of giving new directions, new goals to human
destinies. Why do you deny that?

THOMAS THE CYNIC

Politics still remains the art of the possible. In
the age of mass civilization, the limits of the possible
have been shifted, but they haven't become arbitrary.
The leader who forgets that fact and lets fine phrases

go to his head soon becomes ridiculous. May I remind you of the story of Cola di Rienzo? He rose to control the city of Rome with the support of the priests and the populace, against the nobles who then ruled the roost, exploiting the absence of the Pope, who had moved to Avignon. But when Cola unfortunately wanted to put into practice *quae leggendo didicerat,* what he had learned from reading, he ruined both himself and the cause that he represented. Unaware of the real reasons behind his modest political success and ignorant of the conditions of Italy and Europe at the time, in 1347 he proclaimed the Popular Italian Empire and declared Rome once more the capital of the world, inviting Ludwig of Bavaria, Charles IV and many other princes to visit it and recognize the new empire. He claimed the right to name the Emperor, and gave himself the somewhat prolix and happily not hereditary title of *candidatus Spiritus Sancti miles, Nicolaus severus et clemens, liberator Urbis, zelator Italiae, amator Orbis et tribunus augustus.* As a result he came to the only possible end: abandoned by the priests and killed by the populace. It's not surprising that in later centuries the figure of Cola di Rienzo was warmly admired by many writers and artists, since his enterprise was essentially rhetorical rather than political. Rhetoric, of course, is inherent to the exercise of power, but the politician makes use of it without allowing it to run away with him, whereby he may be distinguished from the mere professional orator.

PROFESSOR PICKUP

It seems to me that the alliance between Mussolini and D'Annunzio contradicts your theory.

THOMAS THE CYNIC

You picked a very poor example, my dear Professor. There is no clearer confirmation of what I said. There was a great difference in the respective attitudes of Mussolini and D'Annunzio at the most critical moments of the immediate postwar period, especially on the question of the city of Fiume. Do you happen to recall that episode? It's worth going into. In September 1919 D'Annunzio, with the secret support of army and monarchist circles guaranteeing him immunity and covering his rear, led a certain number of Italian soldiers to occupy the city of Fiume and to prevent its being ceded to Yugoslavia in accordance with the decisions of the Peace Conference. D'Annunzio was given the assignment at the last moment, and the expedition could easily have taken place without him; but to the public it seemed a purely D'Annunzian enterprise. The poet took advantage of this to set up a miniature state in the little Adriatic city under the despotic government of poetry personified, assisted by the other muses. An enormous crowd was stationed permanently under the poet's balcony, because whenever fancy inspired him he would appear and declaim some new message to the peoples of the earth. He also promulgated a constitution in which all the political and social problems of both past and future were solved; only those of the present were left out. In Milan, Mussolini backed D'Annunzio's action, which went undisturbed for sixteen months, as long as it suited the Italian government. In November 1920 the Giolitti government signed the Treaty of Rapallo with Yugoslavia and ordered the evacuation of Fiume. After a show of resistance, the evacuation took place. At that moment Mussolini dropped D'Annunzio, who instead showed signs of wanting to put up a fight.

MR. DOUBLE YOU

An old comrade-in-arms of the poet whom we met in Venice called that episode a betrayal on Mussolini's part.

THOMAS THE CYNIC

It would be more correct to say that in this case politics betrayed rhetoric. But, mind you, had politics behaved differently it would have been betraying itself. You must realize that the Treaty of Rapallo was signed two months after the workers evacuated the factories they had occupied. The impetus of the revolutionary movement showed many signs of being exhausted, and Italian socialism was beginning its disastrous retreat all along the line. The industrialists and landowners, frightened by the recent danger they had narrowly averted, turned in ever greater numbers to the *Fasci*. They counted on the *Fasci* to destroy the workers' organizations, which were now forced on to the defensive, and to withdraw the concessions which the workers had been hastily granted in the preceding years. At the end of 1920, therefore, completely new horizons were opening before Mussolini. Even if he had assumed previous obligations with D'Annunzio, in the new situation they must naturally have seemed gratuitous poetic license to him.

PROFESSOR PICKUP

Still, though their temperaments were different, D'Annunzio and Mussolini were at that time fighting for basically the same cause, as later events proved.

THOMAS THE CYNIC

Must I repeat once more that the spur of the aspiring dictator is power, that of the rhetoretician eloquence? It's obvious that the fascist leader, especially in a Latin country, must make use of the rhetorician, but he must be careful not to let fine words lead him astray. The vicissitudes of D'Annunzio in the postwar period are a textbook illustration of the fact that rhetoric can never play more than a minor role and is unequal to the task of government. Even the political defeat of European socialism may be ultimately traced to the fact that in the last few decades its leaders attached far more importance to Marxist rhetoric than to the workers' real needs. I also find it rash to assert that the rhetorician has to be more coherent than the man of action. Actually, both are coherent, but in different ways, according to their different aspirations. The fascist leader is coherent, as we have said, so long as he doesn't stray from the path that can lead him to power, even if along the way he has to overcome many "incoherences." In his own way, the rhetorician feels he is coherent if he never loses an opportunity to make a fine speech. After Mussolini's "betrayal," D'Annunzio broke off all personal relations with him, ordered his legionaries to leave the *Fasci,* and came to an understanding with the socialist trade unions. He then forced himself, without entirely succeeding, to adapt his rhetoric to the service of the socialist and humanitarian mythology. But in August 1922 when Fascist gangs broke into the Town Hall of Milan—which was then, and had been for many years, under Socialist administration—there was D'Annunzio in their midst, back with the Fascist mob. From the balcony of the building he commemorated the event with one of his eloquent speeches. Was that incoherence? According to the moral sentiments of the ordinary man, it undoubtedly was; but not according to D'Annunzio. A true rhetorician is incoherent only when he is silent.

MR. DOUBLE YOU

Couldn't he have made a speech at an anti-Fascist meeting, deploring the outrage against the city government and vindicating the flouted rights of the people of Milan?

THOMAS THE CYNIC

He couldn't, and again rhetoric is the reason. The D'Annunzian poetic lyre, as his books prove, was richly equipped with harmonious strings praising violence, lawlessness, the triumph of the victors, but it had no strings that could vibrate with human solidarity for the unhappy fate of the vanquished, even if they happened to be his political allies. He had no choice. He behaved in exactly the same way, and again with perfect coherence, a few months later, when Mussolini came to power. D'Annunzio had plotted up to the last moment to prevent this from happening, but, once it had happened, he instantly sided with the victorious dictator.

PROFESSOR PICKUP

To tell you the truth, D'Annunzio doesn't interest us as much as Mussolini.

THOMAS THE CYNIC

Let's go back to the Duce then. His chief qualities are those inferior forms of intelligence known as instinct and cunning. In general, therefore, if the situation is confused and the future uncertain, before committing himself in any one direction he prefers to engage in a little double-dealing. (Whenever he has tried to think out a decision that would be coherent with all his principles, the result has always been unfortunate.) In August 1914, as editor of the Socialist daily *Avanti!*, he upheld the Socialist non-interventionist policy. But he already saw that Italy couldn't remain neutral long; moreover the passive situation of peace was repugnant to that restless political agitator. So, while continuing to write antiwar articles in the paper, he was careful to establish ties with those who were working to bring about Italy's intervention as an ally of the Entente. A rival paper denounced this double-dealing in an article entitled "The Man with Something to Hide." This forced Mussolini into the open and made him come out hastily in favor of war.

After the war, at the time when everyone in Italy was expecting a proletarian revolution, he speculated simultaneously on the defeat of socialism and on its victory. In September 1920, when the metallurgical workers, followed by workers in other industries, occupied the factories and many people thought that now nothing could stop the revolutionary impetus of the working class, Mussolini—as I said before—wasted no time. He asked to speak with the committee that led the movement and he declared to them: "I am following the occupation of the factories with sympathy. I don't care whether the factories belong to the owners or to the workers. The important thing is the moral renovation of the nation's life." But when the movement failed, and the propertied classes, forgetting their fear, grew arrogant, Mussolini rose up against the "attempt to hurl Italy into the abyss of Bolshevism," and offered himself to the industrialists as savior of the country from the "Asiatic menace of socialism." After winning power he gradually liquidated all the other parties, with the double-dealing game which he himself defined as "the olive branch and the cudgel." I'll give you just one example. Cesare Rossi, head of the Fascist government's press office, has revealed that in July 1923, Mussolini ordered the Fascists of Florence, Pisa, Milan, Monza and other smaller localities to destroy all the offices of Catholic associations during the night. At the same time, according to a document published by the historian Salvemini, Mussolini sent a telegram to the prefects, or chief administrators, of those provinces asking them to convey to the local bishops the Fascist government's regrets on the barbarous damage caused. When Mussolini transferred to the international field these tactics which had been so fruitful in internal politics, he succeeded easily in checkmating the League of Nations. If you were carefully to correlate General De Bono's account of the war in Abyssinia with the temporizing policy of the Fascist envoy in Geneva, you would see that the apparently conciliatory proposals made in Geneva invariably coincided with new war measures. No one can deny that the trick worked, and if it weren't for the poor Abyssinians, I couldn't help rejoicing that certain English politicians, who had been so ready to shower help and praise on Mussolini as long as he confined himself to practicing his art of governing on the poor Italian democrats, should have had to learn his conception of loyalty at their own expense.

PROFESSOR PICKUP

Hindsight easily draws pictures in which everything is logical and foreseen. But perhaps when a man
is at grips with reality, his behavior is less certain.

THOMAS THE CYNIC

Yes, in moments of risk, one has to grope one's
way, with one's eyes glued to the movements of one's
opponents. An escape route must be kept open in case
of unforeseen complications. But all the prudence in
the world can't prevent mistakes and losses. I think
one can discern them at every important turning-
point in Mussolini's career. In fact one may say, without fear of generalizing, that in every phase of its development Italian Fascism has always ended up by
taking the opposite direction to the one foretold by its
leader. However, he has been clever enough to give in
every time, sacrificing his vanity to his ambition. Let
me just tell you about two episodes of this kind. At
the end of 1920 Mussolini thought that Fascism would
remain an exclusively urban movement, and instead,
without his knowing it, Fascism was spreading into
the rural areas. In the summer of 1921, Mussolini saw
that Fascism was no longer an obedient instrument in
his hands. He launched an appeal for a "return to its
origins" and made a peace treaty with the Socialist
Party. The *Fasci* of the agrarian provinces rebelled,
the peace treaty was annulled, and Mussolini adapted
himself to the situation. The following year he himself
expressed contempt of the "idealistic" Fascists who
wanted to return to the party's origins. "To go back
to the party's origins, as certain people want, would
mean declining into infantilism or into senility," he
wrote. "Fascism is, and must be, the organized expres-

sion of this tendency of the contemporary spirit, this classic renewal of life against all destructive races and disruptive theories."

MR. DOUBLE YOU

May I interrupt you? What does "classic renewal of life" mean?

THOMAS THE CYNIC

Nothing. The adjectives "classic" and "historic" in Italian political language are mere pleonasms used to lend distinction and solemnity to a speech. If we were in Italy now, our distinguished professor could interrupt me and say, "At this historic moment, contemplating this classic landscape . . ."

PROFESSOR PICKUP

Instead, I shall merely observe, more prosaically, that the ideological indifference you have just described can be found in Mussolini but not in Hitler.

THOMAS THE CYNIC

No, to a different degree, it can be found in Hitler too. In this respect both dictators faithfully mirror the weaknesses of their respective countries, It seems to me that in the culture of the average Italian, the concepts of history, state, church, society, nation, race, are far clearer and more differentiated than in that of the average German. It's true that the Germans have had Karl Marx and Max Weber, from whom cultivated people in every country have learned a great deal. But the Germans have also had (to speak only of recent times) Stefan Georg and Spengler, whose pseudo concepts are inconceivable outside of the German intellectual autarchy. And, for his part, Hitler, from the earliest days of his National Socialist propaganda, was able to use a certain number of popular prejudices concerning blood, honor, fate, and such things, and exploit them to the utmost, even though such concepts are mythological rather than political. But for the rest, he, too, has proceeded with unscrupulous empiricism. Just as by November 1920, Mussolini already had to abolish the thirteen demagogical points adopted as the Fascist program in March 1919, so Hitler didn't respect the twenty-five points adopted as the program of the NSDAP in February 1920, for very long. The many shifts in the meaning attributed to the word "socialism" in Hitler's propaganda, as the Nazi movement developed, could serve as a starting point for anyone wanting to study the various metamorphoses of Nazi ideology in the period before the Nazis achieved power. Isn't it rather significant that today, in the year of grace 1939, it should be strictly forbidden in both Italy and Germany to publish the original platforms of the parties now in power?

PROFESSOR PICKUP

Well, come to think of it, nobody ever did speak to us about them, either in Rome or in Berlin. Still, Mr. Cynic, there's something that doesn't satisfy me in what you say. By reducing fascism to mere expediency you end up by reducing its historic importance to zero.

THOMAS THE CYNIC

The importance of events has always been independent of the awareness of their protagonists and also—one may as well admit it—of the invective of their victims. Both the ancient Romans and the modern Britons succeeded in creating two powerful empires without any previous plan, almost without noticing what they were doing, and with very little rhetoric. What will be the historical consequences of Fascism and National-Socialism? It's not easy to say. But one can decide whether to support or oppose these dictatorships without having to wait for the answer.

11.

Concerning disgust with the totalitarian vocation and nostalgia for private life.

MR. DOUBLE YOU

Today we'll have to get along without our censorious professor of pantautology. He's gone into town to attend to various matters connected with the remainder of our trip. All things considered, this stay in Switzerland, though it wasn't included in my itinerary, hasn't turned out so badly. Public life here may be dull, but private life is enviable.

THOMAS THE CYNIC

And that's why being Swiss is not so much a nationality as a profession. A man is Swiss just as he might be an engineer or a photographer.

MR. DOUBLE YOU

Last night I had dinner with the family of a Swiss I used to know when I was young. He owns a splendid farm a little way out of town. Although he's rich, his house is modest, almost austere. All evening long he talked to me about nothing but raising livestock and new methods of grafting fruit trees. His daughters waited on us at table. The house was filled with silence and the smell of new-mown hay. I can't help feeling quite envious whenever I think about it.

THOMAS THE CYNIC

That's only human—all too human. Forgive me if I ask you something. Do you often feel a longing for a completely private life?

MR. DOUBLE YOU

Oh, no. Mercifully not.

THOMAS THE CYNIC

It would be nothing to be ashamed of. But be on your guard, it's an inevitable temptation, and you won't be able to shake it off for a long time to come.

MR. DOUBLE YOU

I know that I'd suffocate outside politics, like a fish out of water. It would be a kind of suicide for me.

THOMAS THE CYNIC

But in cases like yours, the temptation can be more insidious. It won't suggest you give up your political career completely, but just that you make a few legitimate concessions to the rights of the private man. Be warned, however. If the aspiring dictator should let normal affections gain the slightest foothold in his heart, he will run the risk of losing his distinctive character and sinking to the level of democratic politicians. May I pursue this subject for a moment? You see, after his first partial victories, which will already have made him an important figure, the aspiring dictator may be tempted to accept a position in the existing system and settle down to a life of safety. A bird in the hand, he may say, is worth two in the bush. But only a fool would reason that way. The logic of the machinery he has set in motion cannot allow such a thing, and if he gives up the struggle for his totalitarian goal, he quickly loses even that little he has already achieved. This should be quite clear:

like all temptations, the temptation to compromise
never keeps its promises. The destiny of the aspiring
dictator is all or nothing.

MR. DOUBLE YOU

If I remember my catechism rightly, it says that
the Lord never tempts a man beyond his endurance.

THOMAS THE CYNIC

Still, it isn't necessary to paint the devil uglier
than he is in order to resist him. Shall we take advantage of the Professor's absence to speak of this sincerely? For instance, you know how the last temptation of Saint Anthony is generally depicted? Various
medieval painters have handed down the image of the
hermit saint assailed by revolting monsters. Rather
naïve of them. It hardly requires great virtue to refuse
to let oneself be persuaded or seduced by monstrous
apparitions. Instead, let's imagine our old hermit with
a fever, lying on a heap of sand. The Evil One appears
to him disguised as a pious pilgrim and speaks to him
in this way: "Poor old man, you came into the desert
to pray, and all these aches and pains of yours are pre-
venting you from doing it the way you would have
liked. You came here to meditate, and your fever
keeps you from concentrating. And besides, here in
the desert, your saintliness isn't serving as a good example to anyone. Who can see you here? Try to be
reasonable: don't you think it would be closer to
God's wishes if you came back to live among men?"
To save himself, the sainted hermit has to cover his
ears and refuse to argue. The mystic's vocation
doesn't admit the voice of common sense. It is essentially inhuman and irrational, it is absolute love of

God. The political vocation, in the extreme form personified by the aspiring dictator, is of the same nature.

MR. DOUBLE YOU

I don't claim to be a political saint, but I can't be
swayed by sentimental arguments—you can be sure
of that.

THOMAS THE CYNIC

Don't be presumptuous, I beg you. Others, whose
existence now seems inconceivable to us outside of
the political area, have hesitated. I need only remind
you of Lenin. . . .

MR. DOUBLE YOU
Not Lenin?

THOMAS THE CYNIC

Yes, his wife tells in her memoirs how Lenin,
during his exile in Geneva after he had broken off
with the Menshiviks, went through a period of severe
depression and considered abandoning politics for-
ever.

MR. DOUBLE YOU
He would have done humanity a great service.

THOMAS THE CYNIC

Do you think so? Hitler's example fits your case
better. In 1922, when the *Völkische Beobachter*—
still a weekly—was gradually enlarging its readership
and had reached a circulation of twenty thousand cop-
ies, Hitler wrote to some friends: "I don't ask much
of life. I would be satisfied if the movement went on

and I could earn my living as editor of the *Völkische Beobachter*." The humble Viennese house painter thought he had "arrived" because he could finally boast of having an intellectual profession. Luckily for him, the onrushing tide of events swept him farther and higher than he had expected. And he was prompt to adapt himself to the ever vaster horizons that kept opening before him. Along the way he rid himself of the secret aspirations left over from the years of his unhappy childhood: the desire to marry a nice girl of good family, to have an intellectual profession respected by public opinion, a comfortable house in the country, a peaceful private life. He arrived where he is now because he was able to give these things up in time and concentrate all his aspirations on the desire for total power. If he had stopped halfway, he wouldn't even be a newspaper editor now; he'd be in jail.

Mussolini ran even more serious risks before he realized that Fascism was a totalitarian movement. I've already mentioned these in the last few days, but I think it would be useful to go into greater detail. Between May and September of 1921, Mussolini tried to transform the Fascist movement into a party of the traditional type by giving up the method of terrorizing his opponents and by making a peace treaty with the Socialists. The attempt failed because the majority of the *Fasci* rebelled and declared that they were prepared to continue the struggle without Mussolini and, if necessary, against him. What had happened? During the second half of 1920 and the early months of 1921, contrary to all the expectations of the Duce, who had written that Fascism would remain an urban movement, Fascism had expanded into the rural

areas of the Po valley and Tuscany, instigating a reign
of terror against the Socialists, particularly those of
the moderate wing. Quite independently of the Duce's
modest political plans, Fascism had found its "true"
vocation as an instrument of the campaign in which
both landowners and industrialists were determined
that the Socialists should be wiped out. It was a local
or, at most, a regional war, not only in its practical
results but also in its inspiration and leadership.
Fasci were set up, multiplied, and took action without awaiting orders from the Party's central office.
Those same capitalists who were financing and arming
the Fascists against the local trade union or coopera-
tive, at the same time continued, on the political level,
to support the Liberal or Conservative parties. In the
spring of 1921 Mussolini realized that Fascism, in
growing to such vast dimensions, had slipped from
his hands. It hadn't become the political instrument
he had wanted, and its acts of violence—which he always publicly approved and encouraged—were, in
practice, being used for other ends and with results
different from what he would have preferred. In that
development of Fascism outside his control, in that
"degeneration" of Fascism from a patriotic movement
to a capitalist militia, Mussolini mistakenly thought he
saw the beginning of its disintegration and of its
speedy end.

May I give you a few quotations? "What happened to the Socialist party in November 1919 is happening to us too, and it was inevitable," Mussolini
wrote toward the end of May of that year. "Fascism
is now the hiding place for the notorious cowards
who were afraid of the others and then afraid of us.
Fascism has been infiltrated by greedy egoists incapa-

ble of sharing in the spirit of national reconciliation. And then, of course, there are those who exploited the prestige of Fascist violence for their petty
personal aims or who are transforming violence as a
means into violence as an end in itself." By "national
reconciliation" Mussolini meant a peace treaty between the *Fasci* and the Socialist organizations which
would put an end to the national guerrilla warfare
and permit the setting up of a coalition government
including what he called "the three effective forces in
the nation," the Socialists, Catholics and Fascists. The
Duce was in a hurry to consolidate the political results of Fascist action because he foresaw that public
opinion would turn against his movement, and if he
didn't make a compromise immediately with the other
political forces, it would soon be too late. During the
month of July negotiations began between Fascist and
Socialist representatives, and on August 2 a pact was
signed in which the two groups agreed to stop using
violence in political and union battles. But the majority of the *Fasci* rebelled against Mussolini and refused
to recognize this pact. A period of violent arguments
followed, in the course of which Mussolini realized
that his authority over his own followers had become
very slight. I think I should read you part of an article
he wrote in his newspaper at that time, to give you an
idea of how little he understood Fascism then:

"For me, Fascism is not an end in itself," he
wrote, "but a means to reestablish a national equilibrium, to revive certain neglected values. These goals
have now been largely achieved. Fascism can now
split, disintegrate, splinter, decline, disappear. If
heavy blows are needed to hasten its destruction, I
will lend myself to this ungrateful task. When Fas-

cism is no longer liberation, but tyranny; when Fascism is no longer the champion of the nation, but the defender of private interests and the most narrow-minded, squalid and petty classes in Italy; when Fascism assumes this form, it will still be Fascism, but not Fascism as I conceived it in one of the saddest moments of our country . . . Did no one see the circle of hate that threatened to stifle good and bad Fascism together? Did no one realize that Fascism—even among the non-socialist classes—had become a synonym of terror?

"I have broken that circle," he went on, "I have cut an opening in the barbed wire of that hate, of the now untrammelled exasperation of vast sections of the population. That hate, that exasperation would have defeated us. I have given Fascism opportunities, I have pointed the way to every kind of greatness with a civil truce that the higher forces both of the Nation and of Humanity demanded. And now they are training on me—just as in the squabbles of the old parties—the heavy artillery of polemics and defamation. They talk of renunciation, capitulation, betrayal, and other similar, sad nonsense . . . Can Fascism do without me? No doubt it can. But I can also do very well without Fascism."

The speech seemed clear—an ultimatum in fact. Meanwhile the opposition to him, led by Dino Grandi, was taking over the most important provincial organizations, whose representatives met in a national conference. Mussolini was roundly condemned as a turn-coat. There are two solutions, they declared: one is parliamentary, the other national. Mussolini is for the parliamentary compromise; we are for the national solution.

Could Fascism have done without Mussolini? It's impossible to say. But obviously he couldn't have done without Fascism, unless he had wanted to risk reverting to the life of a mediocre journalist. In fact, within less than two months, the Duce capitulated, accepting the policy his opposition wanted, namely to continue the terroristic fighting. It was not the last time that this was to happen to him.

MR. DOUBLE YOU

Why didn't the deomocratic parties exploit that disagreement?

THOMAS THE CYNIC

They didn't understand how serious it was. They obstinately went on measuring new events with old yardsticks.

12.

Concerning the dangers of conspiracies and revolts without the support of the police and the army.

THOMAS THE CYNIC

In your biography of Mr. Double You, Professor, I read with particular attention the pages that praised his fearless behavior in the war. Mind you, I too admire courage, but the courage of an aspiring dictator should have nothing romantic or impulsive about it.

PROFESSOR PICKUP

I'm afraid you've taken my story too literally.

THOMAS THE CYNIC

So much the better if I have. It will be that much easier for me to expound my ideas on this subject. An aspiring dictator's courage in the case of civil war is generally demonstrated by the icy calm with which he exposes both his followers and his opponents to danger while remaining in a safe spot himself—without seeming to do so, of course. One must remember that in civil war, as in wars between nations, an ever clearer separation has been established, with the passing of centuries, between the respective duties of the leaders and the led. Among other consequences, greater safety is now ensured those in command. Though this condition is imposed by the vast scale of modern warfare, it is still not entirely accepted by popular opinion, which goes on displaying the same attachment toward authority that children feel for their parents. What parents would leave their children

alone in a moment of danger? What children would
not be panic-stricken, if abandoned by their parents?
This explains the care taken by war propagandists to
dramatize the rare and comfortable visits made to the
front by chiefs of state, with large parties of courtiers,
journalists and photographers. We all remember the
picture of the king in uniform urging the infantry to
attack the enemy trenches, or that of the president of
the republic, in a trench under steady enemy fire,
sharing a private's rations and saying he never ate anything more tasty, or the tragic fate of the prime minister's automobile, struck by a bomb and blown to bits
in an air raid, at a moment, however, when the prime
minister happened to be somewhere else. These leg-
ends, intended to boost the nation's morale, have always been countered by the invectives of the antimilitarists against "generals who die in their beds."
Militarists and antimilitarists both speculate on this
same popular sentiment, which is hardly compatible
with war in its modern form. Civil or guerrilla warfare is no different; it brings to political struggles the
methods, customs and deceits of international conflicts. Wherever this happens, fascism can almost always get the upper hand of the opposing parties,
thanks to some of its characteristics and with the help
of other circumstances which I'd like to outline to
you.

First of all, you must bear in mind that democratic parties, like workers' organizations in general,
are made for times of peace and for peaceful ends.
The only battles they are equipped for are the paper
fights of election periods. Thus it happened that both
in Italy and in Germany eminent political personages
withdrew at the first indication that the political

struggle was degenerating into armed conflict. Their colleagues who stayed in the arena, arguing and discussing as in the good old days, looked ridiculous and pathetic, old-fashioned, outdated characters, like soldiers going into a modern war with shields and spears. In the topsy-turvy postwar society these men were out of place. Their real or imagined qualities (experience of public affairs, knowledge of economic problems, familiarity with foreign countries) were dismissed with contempt. The old politicians didn't know how to harangue effectively at street-corners; they didn't realize that today's loudspeaker demands a new way of speaking, and consequently of thinking. Their complaints that politics was becoming vulgar are reminiscent of Ariosto's invectives against the invention of the blunderbuss. But the Fascist leaders proved to be made of very different metal. They were a product of the war. And their followers, too, were veterans, ex-volunteers, unemployed ex-officers, all of them unsuited to living in peacetime conditions. For them politics was a way of prolonging the war under different conditions, a combined action of violence and propaganda. But it was a war *sui generis* which couldn't be waged by the kind of general who taught in military academies. It wasn't even necessary for the leader to be a war hero. To establish contact and trust, he had only to be a man bitterly disillusioned about the way the war had ended and unable to reconcile himself to the new state of things, above all a man who had, as we say, a devil driving him.

PROFESSOR PICKUP

Surely, Mr. Cynic, you don't mean to cast doubt on the dictators' valiant deeds, the wounds that Mussolini and Hitler received in the war?

THOMAS THE CYNIC

In 1914 and 1915, Mussolini was one of the most active promoters of Italy's intervention on the side of the Entente. But when the war broke out and many young men converted by his propaganda went off as volunteers, he waited until he was called up. He was at the front for exactly thirty-eight days. He was wounded in a commonplace accident during grenade practice, and as soon as he recovered he went back to Milan, where he remained safely until the end of the war. Hitler on the other hand felt stifled by order and peace and had longed for the war to come. He tells in *Mein Kampf* that during the long waiting his heart was filled with nostalgia for the heroic ages when men fought uninterruptedly. So it's easy to imagine that the outbreak of war seemed to him a particularly benevolent gesture on the part of Providence, intended personally for him. He volunteered, but was rejected because of a weak constitution; later he was accepted and used as a liaison corporal at a regimental headquarters. He never, therefore, had a chance to take part in active fighting. The Iron Cross, first class, was awarded him for an episode without a trace in the history of his regiment and which none of his fellow soldiers can remember.

What does it matter? It isn't at all necessary, I repeat, for the fascist leader to perform daring actions; in fact, it's preferable that his spirit of prudence and self-preservation should never desert him for a single instant, so that he won't risk himself or his movement in foolhardy ventures. I admit that for swaying crowds and intimidating the opposition, it's useful for the leader to be known as a man of mettle, fearless in the face of danger, always ready to make the supreme sacrifice for the salvation of his country and of civilization. But this reputation is a matter of smart propaganda. If the legend of the Leader's contempt for danger catches on among the masses and with the opposition, it's only natural that the leader himself, in complete good faith, should end up believing it and becoming a really courageous man at last. But from that moment, new dangers confront him—the dangers of arrogance and imprudence, which may lead to his ruin.

PROFESSOR PICKUP

The fascist leader's courage needn't necessarily be physical. Physical courage is an utterly primitive quality. The Leader's courage is essentially educational, I might almost say priestly. You needn't smile. Didn't you say several times that we are in an epoch of wars and civil wars? Well, the first duty of a leader is to familiarize his own people with the image of death. Once upon a time this was the duty of the priests, but they are no longer in a position to fulfill it—a fact to which the social chaos of today may be ascribed. Don't think for a moment that mass civilization shrinks from the sense of death. Not at all. But it requires a suitable liturgy. Italian Fascism's black pennants and macabre symbols are excellent examples of this. "Live dangerously," that marvelous Fascist maxim, means just that. Basically, the greatest weakness of democracy and socialism in our time is this: they are both epicurean ideals. But in a tragic period like our own, where can a hedonistic ideal lead? Obviously to an increase in the number of deserters. This explains why, whenever there was a clash between a mass of socialist workers and a little squad of fascists, the mass instinctively fled because, as someone remarked, it was made up of people trained to live and not to die. Could you perhaps tell me what place is occupied by the thought of death in democratic or socialistic ideologies? They are purely political ideologies which offer no guidance on the question of man's destiny. But how can you make men face death willingly if they have been taught only to live, and to live in comfort?

MR. DOUBLE YOU

Don't exaggerate, my friend. You know perfectly well that there are brave men in every party, socialist and democratic parties included.

PROFESSOR PICKUP

I'm aware of that, but I doubt that their ideology has ever offered them any moral support at crucial moments. Those who weren't seized with despair in the face of death were probably consoled by some remnant of religious feeling that had lingered in a crevice of the heart. Fascism, on the other hand, is open exaltation of sacrifice. War alone, Mussolini has said, can bring all human energies to the point of maximum tension and leave the stamp of nobility on those who have the courage to face it. War for a man, he added on another occasion, is like maternity for a woman. A short while ago, when I hinted at my skepticism about Mr. Double You's suitability for leading terrorist gangs, I was thinking primarily of his lack of the religious sense of sacrifice. Remember that even Karl Marx had a glimmer of this feeling when he spoke of violence as the "midwife of history."

THOMAS THE CYNIC

Observe, my dear Professor, that he said "midwife," not "mother," and still less "father." In the specific case of Fascism, it can easily be shown that its violence did not give birth to a new society, but on the contrary tried to kill the embryo of a new order which modern society was carrying in its womb. The result therefore was not a birth, but a tragic abortion.

MR. DOUBLE YOU

Would you two mind dropping the gynecology and getting back to politics?

PROFESSOR PICKUP

Vita hominis militia est. Heroism is never useless, even if its utility isn't always of a materialistic kind. From heroism myths are born. But even if the heroism goes unrecorded, it carries its own reward. In this sense fascist heroism proves to be purer and more disinterested than Christian heroism, because the Christian martyr who gives his life for the Faith hopes to conclude a profitable transaction by earning eternal happiness. The fascist martyr, on the contrary, has no extra-terrestrial hopes. His religiosity is more pure.

MR. DOUBLE YOU

You believe in art for art's sake? If one of these days they stop talking back home and start shooting in the streets, I hope it'll be my turn to have some smart followers who'll be able to put up a stiff fight.

PROFESSOR PICKUP

Why should your followers fight to get *you* into power rather than somebody else?

MR. DOUBLE YOU

They'll be paid. If I win, they'll be given jobs.

PROFESSOR PICKUP

Do you honestly believe there are many men prepared to fight a long, bloody civil war merely for money? If they die, what good is your money to them?

MR. DOUBLE YOU

It wouldn't be the first time such a thing happened. That's the fate of mercenaries.

PROFESSOR PICKUP

That's where you're wrong. Your weak spot again: you feel contempt for your fellow man. Even the lowest mercenary, when risking his life for the man who pays him, needs to delude himself about the motive that has led him to this sacrifice. Otherwise he pockets his enlistment money, and when things get dangerous, he deserts or joins the enemy. Remember this: you can't organize a civil war without giving your supporters an overpowering reason to die. I am referring mainly to the shock troops, those that might be called the volunteer suicide squad.

MR. DOUBLE YOU

And what do you suggest as a narcotic for my volunteers?

THOMAS THE CYNIC

May I answer that question? I would suggest the same drug that incited fanatics who have been responsible for massacres in every age, most recently of all

in Italy and Germany, namely idolatrous self-identifi-
cation with the Leader and with the myth that he
personifies. Those whom life has defeated, the men
for whom existence no longer has meaning or value
and yet who shrink from suicide because their despair
isn't personal and because they are full of a vitality
which demands an outlet in some challenging test—
these are the ideal recruits for the impresarios of terrorism. For them totalitarian politics is like opium.
They don't become altogether indifferent to money,
but their reckless courage in street fighting, as our
professor rightly pointed out, depends on something
else. Money, food, alcohol, women, existed before
the war too, and yet phenomena such as Fascist gang
violence and the National-Socialist stormtroopers
would have been absolutely inconceivable then. In
those days the suitable human material was lacking;
men were still individuals with traditional or personal
ideals. Mass civilization and war had not yet yielded
their fruits.

MR. DOUBLE YOU

But mass civilization and war aren't a fascist monopoly.

THOMAS THE CYNIC

That explains many of the complications in recent civil wars. I'd like to point out the main ones. In
the first place, much of the past is still there; it's obviously not entirely wiped out. In the second place,
the established institutions, though discredited, are not
passive or resigned. And finally, the fascists have no
monopoly of fighting spirit; there is plenty of it to be
found on the other side too, especially among those
antifascists whose organization is equally totalitarian.

MR. DOUBLE YOU

And yet in Italy the solution came about quickly.

THOMAS THE CYNIC

Because there the established institutions were very prompt to come down on the side of Fascism.

MR. DOUBLE YOU

Did they suffer from a suicide complex?

THOMAS THE CYNIC

They deluded themselves that Fascism wasn't going to last long and would merely be helpful in restoring order.

MR. DOUBLE YOU

They would have made better use of their remaining energies if they had done something about their own safety.

THOMAS THE CYNIC

Both officially and because of their inherent function the established institutions had their hands tied by the law. In a society in upheaval, the old liberal law makes things easy for subversion. Increasingly large units of the army, the police, the magistrature and the civil service begin first secretly, then openly, to support the Fascist Party. The alibi of these officials is that since they are rendering a service to their country, they may be breaking the letter of the law but they are obeying its spirit. With the *de facto* protection of the institutions it plans to destroy, Fascism can face its opponents and immediate rivals in a condition of overwhelming superiority. Mind you, I'm not repeating antifascist insinuations or assumptions. After the March on Rome, the very people concerned (army officers, police chiefs, judges) did not hesitate to boast of the services they had rendered. The most important episode, from many points of view, occurred when the War Ministry sent a colonel, an expert in matters of civil war, round all divisional headquarters to give timely instruction in ways and means of helping the Fascist movement. The report presented by the colonel on completing his mission was later made public and has never been denied.

Let's take a look at Germany. The first National Socialist nucleus was conceived by the Munich Reichswehr as a political movement and created by Hitler and Röhm. This was in 1921. Germany was then full of freebooting militia organizations: the Erhardt Brigade, the Baltic Landswehr, the Neydebreck Hunters, the Freie Korps of Pfeffer, Rossbach, Loewenfeld and Epp, to name a few. Hitler got his political apprenticeship in the Reichswehr, where just after the armistice he took a course in political instruction and picked up many of the tactical ideas that later proved of such great use to him. First of all, he learned that the support of the masses is always a result of the simultaneous use of propaganda and violence. But it would take too long to go into details now. The collaboration of the armed forces can be found in the history of all dictatorial enterprises, at all times and in all places.

MR. DOUBLE YOU

In our country—I'd better tell you this right away—we unfortunately haven't yet reached that point. I can count on the friendship of a few officers, but the help I get from them doesn't amount to much,

and I doubt whether the higher authorities know anything about it.

THOMAS THE CYNIC

If that's so, then your time is not yet ripe. It's
quite inconceivable that any fascist movement should
gain a foothold, much less make progress, unless the
whole State machinery is paralyzed, leaving important
organs of the executive—particularly those, such as
the police and the army, whose political conscience is
usually more alert—to act independently.

PROFESSOR PICKUP

The paralysis of the government can't have been
as widespread as you say, considering that special laws
were made against Fascism in Italy and Nazism in
Germany. The truth of the matter is that repressive
measures have never prevented revolutions.

THOMAS THE CYNIC

The special laws were passed by parliaments in
which democrats, socialists and communists constituted the great majority. The laws provided for dis-
armament, the prohibition of private military formations, special punishments for those who fomented
hatred among the citizens. But you mustn't forget
one detail, which is that the enforcement of the
laws, decrees and special ordinances was entrusted to
a police force, an army and a magistrature which were
already largely fascist. So that, in practice, the laws
designed to combat the fascists were in the best of
cases a dead letter; but more often, they were me-
ticulously applied against the antifascists. I won't cite
examples because you will find them *ad abundantiam*

in every chronicle of Italian and German politics in the postwar period. The experience of "democratic" legislation against fascism would alone suffice to prove —if proof were needed—that laws are liberal or anti-liberal according to how they are applied.

MR. DOUBLE YOU

I've read a number of bloodcurdling descriptions of the horrors of civil war in various European countries during the last decades. But they are almost always denunciations written by the victims and their friends, so one can't help doubting their veracity.

PROFESSOR PICKUP

Nothing surpasses the barbarity of Bolshevik violence.

THOMAS THE CYNIC

Professor Pickup, you just missed a good opportunity to assert, pantautologically: terror is always terror. This maxim now holds good both for international wars and for the so-called civil ones. In a book by Major General Fuller I read a statement to this effect: the new technique of war is based on the principle of terror; its aim is to inspire terror and to drive the enemy raving mad, at least temporarily.

Terror begins when the conflict no longer outlaws any kind of violence, when there are no longer any rules, laws, customs. Your political opponents break into your house at night, and you don't know what's in store for you. Arrest? Shooting? A mere beating up? Your house burned down? Your wife and children carried off? Or will the enemy be content to amputate your arms? Will they gouge out your eyes and cut off your ears? Will they throw you out of the window? You don't know, and you can't know. That is the whole premise of terror. Terror has no laws or rules. It is pure whim, and its only aim is to terrorize. Its goal is not so much the physical destruction of a limited number of opponents as the mental destruction of the largest possible number—to make them mad, half-witted, abject, to strip them of any remnant of human dignity. As for the promoters and authors of this terror, they too cease to be normal men. The most effective and the most frequent acts of terror are precisely those which one would think the most "useless," the most unnecessary, the most unlikely.

MR. DOUBLE YOU

In Buenos Aires they told me that the dictator of Argentina, the famous De Rosas, had in this respect an inventive genius worthy of a great artist. One morning, for example, strange fruit vendors appeared in the city streets shouting "Fresh peaches," and when shoppers came to buy, the vendors uncovered their baskets and displayed recently severed human heads. It seems that De Rosas had greatly simplified judicial procedure. He concerned himself with the trials personally, but didn't bother to read the testimony. He merely wrote in the margin *cuchillo*, knife, or *bala*, bullet, as his fancy dictated.

THOMAS THE CYNIC

That same De Rosas gloried in his title of "Restorer of the Law," and the slogan that his followers used to chant was, "Long live the holy federation and death to the foul antifederal savages." Today his ferocity is universally deplored, but while he was in power, in the churches of Buenos Aires there were priests who sang solemn *Te Deum*'s in his honor. This weakness, however, isn't only clerical. The violence of our opponents naturally seems fierce, base, inhuman to us, but that of our friends, even when it takes exactly the same form, seems heroic, courageous, idealistic. To my mind, there is nothing more stupid than expressions like "white terror," "red terror," "black terror." The fact of fear-ridden masses has a color that no longer has anything to do with politics.

MR. DOUBLE YOU

Civil war undoubtedly deepens the gulf between the passive majority of the population and the combatant minorities. What you say would be correct, Mr. Cynic, only if you were speaking from the majority's point of view.

PROFESSOR PICKUP

And yet, up to forty or fifty years ago—if you read the history of the working class movement— the masses could produce men bold enough to assassinate monarchs, and groups of men bold enough to fight violently during strikes. How do you explain, Mr. Cynic, the loss of that dynamism, that spirit?

THOMAS THE CYNIC

Perhaps it is one of the consequences of the growth of big industry. Moving from the artisan's shop and the small plant to the great factory, the worker in time undergoes a considerable transformation. His mental horizon is broadened and his class consciousness increased, but at the same time he loses his taste for freedom and his readiness for individual action. The worker in the great factory is apt to be bolder and stronger in mass actions, whether peaceful or violent, whereas he is generally unable to act alone or in a small group. If you look at the newspaper accounts of the anarchist or syndicalist violence which was a frequent occurrence in various countries, including your own, around the final decades of the last century and the beginning of this one, you will see that it was the work of artisans, intellectuals—generally students—or of peasants. If by chance you also find a factory worker, he is probably an ex-peasant or an ex-artisan. The factory worker is the mass-man par excellence. It is no accident that in Italy, Fascism met armed resistance and lost more victims in the regions and cities where large industry doesn't exist and where the workers are employed in small enterprises. Compare the respective attitudes toward fascism of the Spanish workers and the Germans. The difference in national character can explain only in part the different way of reacting to the enemy's attack. The growth of big industry has been a powerful help in reinforcing the tendency of Germans—workers included—toward *zusammenmarschieren*. Their interparty struggles are essentially struggles between different machines. Individual initiative has been reduced to zero.

Another important factor which explains why the workers in big industrial concerns, in Germany but also elsewhere, were at a loss when, after the war, they found themselves faced by fascist terrorism, is that many of them, having been employed in making munitions or in transport or other essential activities, were exempted from war service. It was actually the holders of the so-called "cushy" wartime jobs who, when the war was over, formed the solid core of the workers' organizations. The fact of not having fought in the war, despite their vaunted extremist opinions, separated them from the fascists by a great gulf. They were like men of two different races. In February 1920, in Milan, Mussolini had to face a commission of inquiry to defend himself against the accusations of two former subeditors of his paper. He was accused among other things of having formed terrorist gangs "of mercenaries summoned from Fiume and from various other Italian cities, paid thirty lire a day, plus expenses, and organized for the purpose of intimidation and violence." Mussolini admitted the facts and said to the jury: "All told, there were only a few hundred men, divided into squads commanded by officers, and, of course, all obeyed me. I was a kind of leader of this little army." So there were several hundred mercenaries in the city of Milan alone, going about in groups of three, with nothing to do from morning to night but keep an eye on the opposition, pester its supporters, prepare and carry out attacks, all of which they were paid to do, while the police guaranteed them immunity.

The different social and psychological make-up of the forces which were opposing each other also determined a different technique in attack and defense. The Fascist technique was easily proved superior to that of the opposition. Every act of Fascist violence was answered by the workers either with a protest meeting or a local general strike, according to its gravity. Both of these measures actually caused the people and the authorities considerable annoyance, but they didn't bother the Fascists in the least. The disorganization of public life consequent on the frequent political strikes finally caused increasingly large segments of the population to turn against the workers' organizations. The workers themselves became demoralized and increasingly disinclined to go on strike. I should add that wherever the antifascists formed little squads of their own and procured arms in order to answer violence with violence, the police promptly intervened and disarmed, arrested and tried them. So when the Fascists moved from isolated outrages to collective expeditions over a wider radius, they more and more frequently encountered an unarmed, supine mass, already purged of its more belligerent members. The Fascists thus had easy opportunities to display their heroism. And as the Fascist influence spread, the support of the military authorities became increasingly open and direct. Consequently, the Fascist squads had easy access to arms and munitions. Thanks to special trucks and trains they could move easily from region to region, with tens of thousands of armed men on a war basis, to attack the last cities where their political opponents could still hold meetings openly and publish their newspapers.

MR. DOUBLE YOU

Is it true that among the Fascist squads and the stormtroopers there were quite a few ex-communists?

THOMAS THE CYNIC

Not in Italy. Cases of Italian Communists going over to Fascism were rare and sporadic. Remember that Mussolini came to power in October 1922; Communism was then barely a year old, and though it had been hard hit by civil war, it hadn't yet undergone the demoralizing internal crises that were in store for it later. In Germany, on the contrary, between 1930 and 1933 whole groups of the Communist military organization went, bag and baggage, over to the S.A. But to understand this phenomenon, we must glance at its political background. If you think back now to the policy of the Comintern in Germany up to 1933, you can't avoid the conclusion that it constituted a precious and indispensable aid to Hitler's victory. From 1926 to 1929, as economic activity was rapidly resuming, the Comintern decided that capitalist society had entered the "third period" of its mortal crisis, a period of new proletarian revolutions and revolts during which the communist parties were to concentrate their activity on the planning of general strikes and the struggle for the dictatorship of the proletariat. While in other countries the frequent political shifts of the Comintern aroused little interest except as a news item, Germany at that time was the real field of experimentation for Moscow's tactics. The lunatic theory of the "third period" and of the imminent new revolutionary cycle spurred the German Communist Party to feverish activity, which consisted in provoking clamorous, pseudo-revolutionary incidents. Since the factory workers proved reluctant to take on this task, the German Communist Party, drawing on the vast funds at its disposal, mobilized the unemployed. The Party's "theoreticians" thought to punish the factory workers, who were openly opposed to the new tactics, by deciding that henceforth, in the new era, only the unemployed would represent the true motive force of the revolution, while the workers still employed in factories were to be considered an integral part of the so-called "work-ers' aristocracy" and as such to be distrusted. The Communist Party's military organization therefore got busy provoking "spontaneous" demonstrations and "hunger marches" of the unemployed, and worked out an elaborate strategy for the planning of "sponta-neous" conflicts between the unemployed and the po-lice, which was then in the hands of Social-Democrat ministers and police chiefs. *Oktober*, the Communist Party's politico-military review, collected, analyzed and deduced new rules from the experiences of this cold-blooded guerrilla warfare, and gave minute tech-nical instructions on how to stir up "spontaneous" demonstrations, how to disarm isolated policemen, how to block truckloads of policemen called in as re-inforcements, and other such things. And a slogan was launched against the Storm Troops: "Strike the fascists whenever they cross your path!"

Hardly a day passed without news of bloody clashes between the two military formations, with offices burned and meetings interrupted by the armed adversary. These tactics reached their climax with the "spontaneous" sacking of food shops by groups of unemployed. From the Communist point of view, there would be little to criticize in any of this, if the premise, the notorious theory of the "third period," had been correct and the unemployed had been ac-tively supported by the factory workers and by the sympathy of all the rest of the masses. But, instead, the results were disastrous both for the Communist Party and for democracy. When the crash came, Communism was cut off not only from those workers who still had jobs, but even from the majority of the unemployed who by now were tired and disillusioned by the "imminent" revolution's failure to materialize.

In 1930, to try to regain lost ground the Communist Party made another shift in the party line. Premeditated guerrilla warfare was harshly condemned, and the Party went back to the policy of working to win the votes of the great masses, including those of the recently scorned "working-class aristocracy." At this point, numerous units of the Communist military organization went over en masse to National Socialism, soon adding new laurels to the old, with "spontaneous" attacks on the offices and meetings of their former party. It was a real surprise for the Berliners one day to see the typical Communist *Schalmeien Kappellen* parade through the streets in brown shirts. In North Germany it was hard to find a stormtrooper who hadn't come from the Communist ranks.

The Party's subsequent strategy, however, was to offer National Socialism further aid in winning recruits from the proletariat. The new slogan suggested by Moscow was: "Fight Social-Fascism" (this term referred exclusively to the Social-Democrats and the reform wing of the trade-unionists). "First defeat Social Democracy, then Fascism." The Communist Party tried to stem working-class desertions to National Socialism by competing with the Nazis in patriotic demagogy, demanding the abrogation of the Versailles Treaty, the nonenforcement of the Young Plan, and furthermore—a luxury Hitler couldn't afford—the evacuation of South Tyrol by the Italian invader. The fact of sharing identical slogans actually gave rise to occasions when the two parties collaborated in some specific action. This happened with the plebiscite against the Social Democrat government of Prussia.

Originally the plebiscite had been a National Socialist initiative, and the German Communists had opposed
it, saying it was all political demagoguery. Later, on
orders from Moscow, they supported it, justifying
this behavior on the principle that, to defeat Fascism,
they would first have to tread on the putrefied corpse
of democracy. On that occasion Communist groups
were to be seen in harmonious unison with stormtroopers, forming "speaking choirs" in the court-
yards of the big blocks of workers' flats and in the
streets, urging the electors to vote against the Social
Democrat government. Communists and Nazis had another opportunity to fraternize in 1932, during the
great Berlin transport strike, in which both the National Socialists and Communists took an active part.
After those episodes the S.A. could circulate freely
in working-class neighborhoods, and the gulf that had
previously separated the two supposedly irreconcilable forces, proletariat and National Socialism, appeared to have been closed. The conviction that a defeat, even by Fascism, of democratic institutions
would be per se favorable to the Communist cause
was so rooted in Moscow's followers that at the beginning of 1933, when Hitler came to power, the first
comments of the Communist press did not report
that event for what it was—that is, a dire defeat
for them—but considered it a great step forward toward the final victory of the proletariat.

MR. DOUBLE YOU
It's a shame, a downright shame that the Communist Party in America is so weak. Pickup, if you hadn't
made us waste all that time in Rome and Berlin, we
could have gone to Moscow, and probably persuaded

Stalin to help wake up American Communism. How can I save America from the Red Menace, if the menace doesn't exist?

THOMAS THE CYNIC

Stalin can find other ways to harm Russia's most powerful rival; he doesn't necessarily have to help the American Communist Party. You may be quite sure he wouldn't hesitate to help you, Mr. Double You—with prudence, of course—once he's convinced that you're likely to succeed.

MR. DOUBLE YOU

As I said before, American Fascism doesn't need rubles as much as it needs a good German-style communist party.

PROFESSOR PICKUP

How long are you two going to continue this contest of cynicism?

MR. DOUBLE YOU

We forgot *you* were here. What were we talking about before?

THOMAS THE CYNIC

About how necessary it is to have the army's support at the right moment.

MR. DOUBLE YOU

Oh yes. But later, at the wrong moment, couldn't they get rid of me and take my place?

THOMAS THE CYNIC

Of course they could. As soon as you start win-

ning a battle, you have to be on guard against your allies. So, it might be worth discussing the danger of the
military *coup d'état* for a moment. Personally, I think
it shouldn't be confused with the totalitarian dictatorship typical of our time. The military *pronunciamento*
is unlikely to happen in the more developed countries.
The first obstacle is the diversity of people's political
opinions, each of them reflected in the army. There
would then be the danger of conflicting military sedi-
tions. Furthermore, a military dictatorship would be
utterly incapable of finding a solution—even a tem-
porary one—for the political and social problems at
the root of the disorder. Such a regime can have only
the purely negative function of suspending party battles and waiting for tempers to cool before going
back to the preceding regime—a moderating, care-
taker function. But if the difficulties among politicians
aren't of a personal nature only, if there are grave
questions of a political, economic and social nature to
be dealt with, then the military dictatorship is of no
use at all. It isn't even capable of adopting the kind of
fictitious solution that Fascism delights in. In an emergency situation the army may take power away from
the civilian government by legally proclaiming mar-
tial law. This is a limited provision, not to be confused
with the *coup d'état;* sometimes, in fact, the former is
employed to avert the latter.

Military dictatorship, on the other hand, is more
likely to occur in a socially backward country, a
country where there is no *bourgeoisie* in the modern
sense, or where it is weak, not organized, broken
up into numerous factions with many feudal leftovers. The army, centering around its general staff,
constitutes the most powerful political organism in

such countries, the only central organism with branches throughout the national territory. When an outbreak of disorders coincides with the impotence of the old political cliques, the army may appear, in such countries, to be the only barrier against the so-called anarchy of the masses and the "corruption" of the politicians. The military *coup d'état* has much in common with the palace revolution; among other things, both are prepared in secret and carried out easily and quickly. The only danger for the leaders of a military *pronunciamento* is the subsequent jealousy among rival generals; from the old political parties they have little to fear. A telephone call from the nearest barracks is usually enough to make a politician listen to reason.

MR. DOUBLE YOU

The outline you've just given needs a number of variants—as many as there are countries where a *pronunciamento* could take place.

THOMAS THE CYNIC

All right, then, let's return to the other situation: where the role of the army in politics is limited to assisting the totalitarian transformation of the state. For the reasons already mentioned, the protagonist of this transformation can only be a party, even though the party be *sui generis*. It will need help from at least a part of the army's higher officers, but they must act with a certain amount of prudence. They will dare to take sides openly with the aspiring dictator only when the outcome of the struggle seems to have been decided in his favor. Since you have chosen North and not South America as your theatre of operations, you needn't be too afraid that a general will steal your place, but at the same time you have less hope that he will put entire regiments at your disposal. You can get advice and information from him. You can be given arms, whose disappearance from military arsenals will be attributed to "unknown thieves." Many military men may join your terrorist groups on an individual basis, in order to lead them, but that's all.

PROFESSOR PICKUP

At last you have admitted that there's such a thing as idealistic behavior. Now, please, don't take back your words.

THOMAS THE CYNIC

I'll leave that pleasure to you. But, for the sake of clarity, I wouldn't want you to think that the relationship between army officers and fascists is that of benefactor and beneficiary. It's more complex than that. The Italian army men who were of most help to Fascism at the start became suspicious as soon as they realized by what paths, in what company, and with what voracity Fascism was heading for power. Though officers and Fascists continued to work together, there soon grew up between them an atmosphere of tension and reciprocal mistrust which, one may say, has never ceased. Hilter's intention, at the moment when he laid the foundations of National Socialism, was to march in the footsteps of the Reichswehr, to be, in a certain sense, its propagandist and political adviser. When, encouraged by his first successes, he tried to go ahead on his own and force the Reichswehr to follow him by confronting it with *faits accomplis,* Hitler's disappointment was enormous. The

Reichswehr refused its support. The Butsch of May 1, 1923, and that of November 9 of the same year failed miserably as a result, and for a moment Hitler even contemplated suicide.

PROFESSOR PICKUP

The disagreements you are bringing up seem to me the effect of temperamental differences rather than anything else. Professional soldiers, as we all know, are calm, cold, prudent, whereas the fascist leader is by nature a romantic.

THOMAS THE CYNIC

That theme deserves more serious comment. The aspiring dictator can never be sufficiently warned against the dangers of embarking on conspiracies or revolts without the support of both police and army. Between the first and the second putsch attempted by Hitler in 1923—the failure of which brought him to the brink of desperation—he received a written statement from his friend Scheubner-Richter which contained the following admonition to prudence: "National revolution cannot precede the assumption of political power. On the contrary, possession of the State police machinery is the premise of national revolution. In other words, one must at least attempt to get control of the State police force by apparently legal means, though of course legal means don't exclude a little more or less illegal pressure. . . . The more energetically the operation is pressed forward by popular opinion and the more legal it appears, the less risk there will be." Hitler didn't give this warning the importance it deserved and he was consequently unable to avoid some bitter experiences, which remained a lesson to him for the rest of his life. Ten years later, in the spring of 1932, when the Storm Troop leaders, Röhm especially, persistently urged him to attempt an armed revolt, Hitler refused. The police, he answered, was still in the hands of his opponents. Later, National Socialism had the opportunity in Austria to apply both kinds of tactics, that of armed revolt and that of a political ultimatum preceded by the conquest from within of the enemy's key positions. The results are there for all to see, and leave no doubt as to which of the two devices is superior. Mussolini had the superiority (which I assure you doesn't flatter my national pride) to sense this truth clearly from the very beginning of his movement. He never seriously thought of an armed uprising, even though at various times, to test the reactions of his opponents, he spread the rumor that the Fascists were preparing one. There was the famous Sarzana episode, when five hundred Fascist militiamen, confronted by eight carabinieri and three soldiers, took flight and were pursued by the local population, leaving ten dead and dozens of wounded strewn about in the fields, hanging from the trees or drowned in the streams. This episode proved, to all those who weren't previously convinced of it, that the real strength of the Fascist gangs, without the support of the police and the army, was minimal. Mussolini already knew it. That's why he didn't hesitate to say no to D'Annunzio's invitation from Fiume. When others reproached him for this refusal, Mussolini answered: "I personally have never written or in any way intimated to D'Annunzio that the revolution in Italy depended on my private whim. The revolution isn't a *boîte à surprise* that you can open whenever you like by pressing the button . . . History tells us that revolutions are made with the army and not against the army, with weapons and not without them. . . ."

PROFESSOR PICKUP

What about the March on Rome? How can you reconcile what you have just said, Mr. Cynic, with that Fascist insurrection in every city and the march toward Rome of columns in battle array which Mussolini has made so much of as a dangerous armed operation?

THOMAS THE CYNIC

If it's all right with both of you, we'll talk about that next time.

13.

Concerning "Operation Mess of Pottage" and the coup d'état *with the help of the authorities.*

PROFESSOR PICKUP

Even though hostile propaganda tries to exaggerate the number of victims caused by fascist violence, you must admit, Mr. Cynic, that they are far fewer than those of the Bolshevik revolution.

THOMAS THE CYNIC

If our discussion is to be serious, we must first of all distinguish clearly between a *coup d'état* and a revolution. We'd better use the former term to mean a political change which is not in opposition to the existing social order, whose promoters, in fact, zealously proclaim their desire to restore that order, bring it back, as it were, to its pristine virtues. This, as we have seen, makes it easier to win the support of at least a part of the old governmental machine, and the good will—or at least the acquiescence—of the rest. If along the way, the *coup* has consequences that go beyond what everyone expected, I don't think this can always be imputed to the wiles of the dictator. As for the Fascist or Nazi *coup d'état*, it is distinct from the traditional one in many ways, but above all because it synchronizes conspiracy at the top with strong pressure from the streets.

PROFESSOR PICKUP

My remark wasn't intended to be sentimental; it was just to get the conversation going. For that matter,

I'm quite aware that every step of history drips with blood, and I deplore the fact that education in the schools nowadays neglects to impress this fundamental truth on the minds of the young. It's obvious, too, that the decadence of modern religions is a consequence of their having given up blood sacrifices. If today people on the whole don't go much to church and, when they go, are indifferent to the various liturgical rites, it's because the sacrifice is now only symbolical. The altars of the Lord are no longer shrouded in the smoke of burnt offerings. Incense is just a ridiculous substitute. From the days of ancient sacrifices man has inherited the feeling that bloodshed is the only way to placate the wrath of the supernatural powers and obtain their compassion. Western socialism—surely even you will admit this—has made the mistake of being pacifist. Only those who understand nothing of the secret needs of the common people can find cause for astonishment in the fact that fascism and Bolshevism continue to keep their millions of followers despite all the shedding of blood. The bloodshed isn't their weakness; it's their strength—I mean, their spiritual strength. The leaders make no secret of it, and on all solemn occasions they are fond of invoking the "martyrs of the revolution." They like to recall the fact that the new regime has paid its "blood price" and is therefore following the rule.

THOMAS THE CYNIC

The number of Italian Fascists killed in political conflicts between 1919 and 1926 was about four hundred and fifty. For the same period of time, the number of antifascist dead amounts to about two thousand. Since we are discussing human lives, both figures

are high; but why do the Fascist propagandists feel
they must enlarge the number of their party's victims
and talk constantly of "thousands of Fascist martyrs"? I don't suppose they imagine that with this
endlessly repeated lie they're going to deceive the
gods.

MR. DOUBLE YOU

I'd be interested to hear your version of the
March on Rome.

PROFESSOR PICKUP

What's the use of that? None of us understands
military matters.

THOMAS THE CYNIC

But Professor, an insurrection is always a primarily political operation, and only marginally a military
operation. As for the Fascist *coup d'état*, it was primarily a political operation accompanied by demonstrations and parades of a military type. The use of violence was indispensable to Fascism for terrorizing
Socialists and democrats throughout the country. Once
that job was done, however, it was easy for the Fascists to dislodge the surviving members of the old political class from any ruling positions they were still
hanging on to. The aspiring dictator must be adept at
making the capitulation of the old politicians seem a
brilliant military operation, and he must present himself
to public opinion as Caesar reincarnate. This mystification is all the easier because the fascist pseudo-insur-
rection takes place in an atmosphere of panic and
dread which is very like that of an authentic insurrection.

In his "Letter to the Comrades" written in October 1917, Lenin defined the following as being the conditions which make an insurrection possible: the incapacity of the ruling classes to govern must be evident; there must be general, furious hostility towards the established order; and—for a Communist insurrection—the middle classes must show that they are in sympathy with the revolutionary workers' movement. Trotsky defined the final act of the insurrection as "striking a paralytic with your fist." But true insurrections don't confine themselves to striking down the old, impotent government. They also destroy its machinery of government and replace it with a new one, causing upheaval in political and social relationships among the citizens. Fascism, on the other hand, brings off its *coup d'état* with the assistance of those same authorities who have already helped it to terrorize the country. And when that is done, the leader's fateful march on the capital can take place in a sleeping car.

MR. DOUBLE YOU

To me this sounds like a comic strip. Mind you, I don't mean that as a criticism; I love comic strips.

THOMAS THE CYNIC

But what I meant to point out was this: when the general situation is favorable to insurrection, the aspiring dictator must use his cunning more than his strength. I would like to call your attention particularly to three points. The first is the necessity of reassuring big business in anticipation of the *coup d'état*.

MR. DOUBLE YOU

Are you referring to the old French saying, *L'argent fait la guerre?*

THOMAS THE CYNIC

That's a corollary to what I'm about to say to you.

MR. DOUBLE YOU

Don't worry about money. I'll be able to find that easily enough.

PROFESSOR PICKUP

My dear Double You, this is a surprise to me. Your only financial resources are the donations of some semilegal or completely illegal organizations that run gambling houses, brothels and betting booths. You obviously have no idea of what a *coup d'état* can cost.

MR. DOUBLE YOU

In our previous talks, Mr. Cynic minutely described what's necessary: a combination of circumstances favoring the *coup d'état*. In that situation, I haven't the slightest doubt about how businessmen will behave toward me.

PROFESSOR PICKUP

Are you referring to our great captains of finance? Their caution is proverbial.

MR. DOUBLE YOU

It's precisely their caution I'm counting on. One of the most important men in our sugar industry recently declared, during a trial in Washington, that his company supported the majority party in every state, whichever party it happened to be. He was asked, "And in case of doubt?" "In such cases," he replied, "we finance both parties." So, as I said, when the situation looks promising for me, I won't have to worry about how to raise money.

THOMAS THE CYNIC

Again you embarrass me. I am trying to give lessons to a master.

MR. DOUBLE YOU

You said there were three subjects you wanted to discuss.

THOMAS THE CYNIC

The second might be called the "mess of pottage" operation. It concerns the aspiring dictator's behavior toward the politicians of the old ruling class. In general these are shrewd men, hardened to all kinds of intrigue, believing they have a kind of primogeniture right to power. Their intelligence warns them that their day is over, but they can't resign themselves. Just as a man who is seriously ill will, a few hours before the death agony, suddenly rally, ask for food and drink, recognize his relations, and in general show all those illusory signs of recovery that old peasant women call "the improvement of death." So when a regime's days are numbered, sensing the approach of the end it fires its last remaining shots, it redoubles its compromise offers, its intrigues, its threats, and is seized with a deceptive euphoria. "Well-informed" journalists then spread reassuring news: "Thanks to the government's vigorous stand the danger of a *coup d'état* has been finally averted"; "The Rome government's threat to call out the army against the blackshirts induces Mussolini to give up his march on Rome"; "Minister Schleicher, supported by Hindenburg, the Reichswehr and the Socialist trade unions, blocks all avenues of the National Socialist advance to power"; "The plebiscite decreed by Schuschnigg will be the lasting affirmation of Austria's independence. . . ." A true politician, however, who has seen as much of politics as any old peasant woman has seen birth and death, will instantly realize that all this feverish activity is only the fictitious improvement that shortly precedes death.

PROFESSOR PICKUP

To define this phenomenon, may I suggest the poetic image of the swan song?

THOMAS THE CYNIC

We had that in Italy too. Under the delusion that they were capable of stopping the course of events, a few old politicians, on the eve of the March on Rome, turned to D'Annunzio. His nature, as is well known, is similar to that of the swan. Since there was the chance of making a great speech, D'Annunzio naturally accepted. It was agreed that he would place himself at the head of a veteran's "national reconciliation" movement, and the poet personally set the scene. At the same time, in the corridors of the Chamber of Deputies, known in Italy not without reason as the "halls of lost footsteps," every conceivable cabinet combination likely to intimidate, appease or seduce Mussolini was being investigated. And there were Fascists, too, who persistently urged a compromise, fearing that later on it might be too late.

In 1932 the same situation occurred in Germany when one wing of National Socialism, led by Gregor Strasser, insisted that the movement had already begun its descending curve and should accept a minority role in a coalition cabinet. Hitler wisely refused, just as a few months earlier he had rejected for the last time the suggestions of Röhm and the S.A. leaders for an immediate putsch.

MR. DOUBLE YOU

It's easy to decide now who was right and who was wrong. But events might equally well have worked out differently.

THOMAS THE CYNIC

When things reach that stage, the only possible factor that could still jeopardize everything would be stupidity on your part. You mustn't let yourself be fooled by the blah-blah of the old politicians. Each of them hopes to save himself by sacrificing his friends. Be neither impatient nor brutal nor merciful with them. Pretend to listen to them and leave them up in the air. You will receive offers of collaboration from all sides; various forms of coalition will be proposed to you, plans for national renovation, blueprints for alliances among related groups. They will even think up Committees of Public Safety presided over by neutral personages. You must pretend to take every proposal into consideration, but then you will criticize some of the details. When the project has been revised according to your suggestions, you must declare that meanwhile the situation has changed; then you make new demands. In each group you will foster the illusion that in the inevitable, any-day-now *coup d'état* they will be the only ones saved. Old and respected parliamentary leaders will then be seen publically condemning "all *a priori* prejudice" against fascism, and praising the "youthfulness and dynamism" of the movement. By this time nobody will dare deny your right to take over the government. They will only argue about when to do it, how to do it, and which of your colleagues ought to be ministers. Most people will condemn the last-ditch opposition of the antifascists, saying that they are lackeys of the foreigner. The old political leaders will get public opinion gradually convinced that it's a good idea for the fascists to have a share of the power. You will reject all proposals, but don't remove from the politicians' twitching nostrils that ambrosial mess of pottage: coalition.

PROFESSOR PICKUP

Do you think those old foxes will fall into the trap so easily?

THOMAS THE CYNIC

Yes, I do. They are expert political gamblers; some are even notorious for cheating. But the game that they know to perfection is the old parliamentary one. They are ignorant of the cruel laws of the *coup d'état* and its complicated mechanism. The aspiring dictator toys with them like a cat with mice. Shall I give you an example? In November 1849, Louis Bonaparte declared that he would be satisfied with a cabinet of nonparliamentarians. In January 1851, a cabinet not responsible to an elected body was enough for him. On April 11, he insisted on having a cabinet that would be antiparliamentary. Would you like a more recent case? At the end of January 1933, on the eve of the German elections, Hitler gave his solemn word of honor that he would retain the ministers then in office, whatever the results of the elections. The *coup* of February 27 created a situation in which that promise became valueless. In the meetings of the Hitler-Hugenberg cabinet, as described by Goebbels, nothing was ever discussed or put to a vote; Hitler made the decisions for everybody. In June Hugenberg was sent home. His pottage was finished. In the meantime a more painful fate had befallen the Social Democrats. In the illusion that he was saving the party from being dissolved, that party's leader, Otto Wels, had resigned on March 30 from the executive committee of the Socialist International after it had passed a motion condemning the Hitler regime. On April 27 the party made another attempt at survival, appointing a new group of leaders and warning members to contain their activities within the new legal limits. It was no use. On May 10 Göring had all the Social Democrat party and newspaper offices seized. And as if this weren't enough, on May 17 the Social Democrats sank so low as to approve a speech of Hitler's in the Reichstag about Germany's new foreign policy. Before the speech, the deputies had been warned that to vote against it would involve them in mortal danger. They voted in favor, but the danger remained.

MR. DOUBLE YOU

What was the third subject you wanted to bring up?

THOMAS THE CYNIC

I have to retrace my steps for a moment. In the next-to-last scene of the last act of the *coup d'état* a conspiracy is always uncovered, or else there is an attempted assassination that fills the nation with horror, thus preparing the way to the happy ending.

PROFESSOR PICKUP

Is Providence always so punctual?

THOMAS THE CYNIC

The art of conspiracies and assassinations is rather delicate and cannot be left to chance. The best conspiracies and assassinations are naturally the ones arranged by the police. They alone would suffice to justify the existence of that useful institution. But the aspiring dictator must be ready to exploit the repercussions at once. The plot or conspiracy that works best is the one where the "enemy within," the implacable opponent of private property, of faith and morals, is shown to be in league with the "traditional enemy beyond the border."

PROFESSOR PICKUP

You're forgetting that in our country there's no real communist danger.

THOMAS THE CYNIC

All the better. A false conspiracy, if well publicized, has all the advantages and none of the inconveniences of a real one. Besides, there was no danger of a communist insurrection in Italy in October 1922, or in Germany in March 1933; still Mussolini and Hitler managed to create that danger and promptly exploit it. And they continued to recreate and re-exploit it every time it suited their convenience. "Saving the fatherland from an imminent danger" is such a decisive operation in the technique of every *coup d'état* that it would be unforgivably careless of me not to insist upon it.

When it comes to citing historical examples, there is an embarrassment of riches. The same plan works for any kind of *coup d'état:* Bonapartist, military, fascist and, of course, antifascist. Napoleon Bonaparte had his troops occupy the hall of the Council of the Five Hundred and had himself named Consul "to liberate the majority from a handful of traitors in the service of England." In order, however, to transfer the Councils from Paris to Saint-Cloud and to smooth the way for the *coup d'état*, he had to show that the republic was in danger; this task he gave to President Sieyes. On the evening of December 24, 1800, as Napoleon, now First Consul, was going to the opera house, an infernal machine exploded near his carriage. The police blamed the Jacobins, of whom five were executed and ninety-eight deported to French Guiana. On March 9, 1804, another assassination plot was discovered by the police before it could be put into effect. Napoleon took advantage of it to have the Duc d'Enghien executed, along with a number of other political opponents. This paved the way for the Proclamation of the Empire. The restoration of the Bourbons, to tell the truth, was every bit as good at this sort of thing—for instance, the conspiracies of the "black brooch" and the "Patrists of 1816."

Aspiring dictators should take hope, seeing how these old tricks, which have been exposed a hundred times, still go on easily deceiving the public. The masses—this is the truth of it—are a great beast without memory. In July 1921, polemicizing with the extremists of his own party, Mussolini wrote that in Italy there was no longer a communist danger: "To claim that a Bolshevik menace still exists in Italy is to misunderstand reality. Bolshevism has been defeated." But the following year the communist danger served him as an excuse for his *coup d'état*.

You must give the Germans credit for their genius at turning their every scheme into a system, leaving nothing unforeseen or improvised. Hitler's *coup* was conceived and carried out with the cold precision that is the basis of Prussian military art. "The communist plot" was the keystone of the strategic plan. Röhm's *Memoirs* contain an advance confession. Speaking of the military actions undertaken by the S.A. with a view to the conquest of power, Röhm warned, "Party propaganda must camouflage these actions with a violent communist uprising." This suggestion was heeded and put into practice as soon as the situation seemed ripe.

PROFESSOR PICKUP

In Berlin we were assured that in February 1933 the police discovered tons of conspiratorial material in the basement of the "Karl Liebknecht House" —proof that the communists were on the point of launching an insurrection.

THOMAS THE CYNIC

Several years have gone by since then and that proof has never been published. No German court has ever examined that material. Frankly, it would be superfluous, for it consisted only of newspaper files, collections of monthly reviews, books published abroad as well as in Germany, all of them known to the general public. I suppose your police will have no trouble uncovering stores of suspicious books at the right moment?

MR. DOUBLE YOU

The Library of Congress is jammed with them. What greater proof could there be, for our plain, ordinary citizens, of the treachery of our old governing class?

PROFESSOR PICKUP

What if your opponents insist on the publication of that proof?

THOMAS THE CYNIC

You could even accept the challenge. The huge quantity of suspect material will naturally relieve you of the obligation to publish it in its entirety. It's easy to make any book say what you like by taking a sentence here and a sentence there and then cleverly putting them together. Not even the Holy Bible is safe from this method. You surely know the famous saying; "Give me a single sentence from a book, and I'll have the author hanged on the strength of it." This will also make it easy for you to justify abolishing the freedom of the press. That's what Stalin did when he started liquidating the various hubs of internal opposition with the famous trials based on accusations of plots, plots arranged by the police. His massacre of thousands of opponents, following on the brilliantly staged assassination of Kirov in Leningrad, is a little masterpiece of its kind.

It's useless, however, to invent a conspiracy if it isn't exploited within a few hours. There isn't a moment to waste; the enemy must be taken by surprise. Depending on the situation, the "discovery of the conspiracy" can be used either to hasten the aspiring dictator's seizure of power or to transform the government of public safety, of which he is a member, into a personal dictatorship. Two important conditions are not to be forgotten: the "discovery of the conspiracy" must take place in the capital or its vicinity, and the police must already be controlled by the fascist party. Merely to reveal the existence of the "conspiracy," however, may not always be enough. It may be more effective to show it already in progress, blaming the conspirators for some monstrous assassination that will horrify every honest citizen and arouse in the country a pogrom atmosphere against the "enemy within" and the demand for a dictator with an iron fist, capable of ridding the country of such rabble.

PROFESSOR PICKUP

Now you're going to cite the burning of the Reichstag as an example.

THOMAS THE CYNIC

That was an excellent idea, but it was inefficiently carried out. Be on your guard against the same errors. It's certainly wise to involve a foreigner in the crime, preferably a Slav or at least a man with red hair, so that you can point to the "work of the fifth column." But avoid accusing a real opponent, hardened by emigration and police persecution. In the case of a fire, you must, of course, call the firemen, but the police must prevent them from arriving too soon and making unpleasant discoveries about the origins of the blaze. You have no assurance that the men who are to concoct the crime won't boast of their cleverness later to their friends, so they must be removed from circulation immediately after the event. If you can't avoid a trial dealing with the conspiracy and the crime, it must—at the very least—be held before a special court, so that disobedient defendants or witnesses or lawyers can be eliminated beforehand, and the hearings can have the educational quality of a protest meeting against both the "enemy within" and the "sinister hand of the foreigner."

You can take the Moscow trials as perfect examples of how to administer justice in the service of propaganda. But I don't want to discourage you with all these different sorts of advice; they only concern details. The essential thing, when the whole country is aghast at the news of the crime, is not to waste a minute before seizing full powers. The memory of those moments inspires an epic tone in all the chroniclers of National Socialism. In his diary Goebbels wrote, "Living is a pleasure again at last." And when he reached the scene of the fire, Hitler turned to the Catholic von Papen at his side and exclaimed, "This is a sign from God. Nobody can prevent us now from destroying the communists with an iron fist."

MR. DOUBLE YOU

I'd add a criticism of my own to the ones you've listed. In a situation where parliamentary government already had been completely discredited, couldn't they have burned down some building closer to the people's hearts?

THOMAS THE CYNIC

I congratulate you, Mr. Double You. The problem to be solved is the very one you have indicated: a problem of mass psychology. We have seen whole nations remain indifferent to the news of vast massacres, then tremble at the fate of one innocent man sentenced to death. You mustn't think the most impressive crimes are those with the largest number of

victims. Many friends and supporters of the Paris
Commune who defended and justified the most vigorous measures of that emergency government couldn't
forgive it for trying to knock down the pillar in Place
Vendôme. Victor Hugo, who as a poet had all the
sentimental weaknesses of the common people, called
that superfluous and innocuous gesture "a crime of
lèse-nation" and he bore a lasting grudge against the
communards even after their bloody defeat.

MR. DOUBLE YOU

The example of Place Vendôme gives me some
ideas. What would you say if I allowed the "fifth column" to steal the coffin of the Unknown Soldier? And
if I then arranged that I personally should have the
honor of finding it again in some cave in a photogenic
mountainous landscape? Or what if I had the Statue of
Liberty blown up, blaming it on the same "fifth column"? Strictly between ourselves, that statue has always got on my nerves.

THOMAS THE CYNIC

Those ideas are worth thinking about. The first
would enable you to disguise your March on Washington as an immense patriotic procession organized
with the excuse of accompanying the Unknown Soldier's remains back to their official resting place. The
second would offer the opportunity of having the abolition of political and democratic institutions coincide
with the restoration of the Statue of Liberty. You
could even give yourself a fine title for it: "Mr. Double You, *Restaurator Libertatis.*" This could adorn the
dictator's portrait on the new dollar bills and postage
stamps.

PROFESSOR PICKUP

Before talking about changes in postage stamps, I think we should finish talking about the *coup d'état*. Experience proves that the political maneuvers you have illustrated to us, Mr. Cynic, are not always enough to ensure the seizure of power. For power to be achieved, armed legions must sometimes be made to march on the capital and attack the forces which have remained loyal to the old government.

THOMAS THE CYNIC

The last act of the *coup* (and this is the third subject I wanted to talk to you about) is a military parade. Its only function, however, is to strike fear into any wavering opponents, and also into the nation's constitutional bodies; it has no warlike mission. It's a show of force that is designed to make the use of force unnecessary. Various authors have tried to see a difference between Mussolini's *coup d'état* and Hitler's, because of the fact that in Italy the Fascist troops paraded even before Mussolini was named Chief of State, while in Germany the parade came afterward. But this is not correct.

The blackshirts didn't enter Rome and have their parade until after Mussolini had been received by the King and invited to form a new cabinet. The fact that in Italy it was necessary to intimidate the democratic government in advance by mobilizing the blackshirts and staging a March on Rome is understandable if you must remember that Mussolini found himself faced with the problem of power barely two years after the foundation of the *Fasci*. Hitler, on the other hand, came to power after twelve years, when the demoralization of his opponents was more advanced and the

S.A. had already been recognized by the "democratic" government as auxiliary police troops. In both cases, however, the change of government proceeded along formally legal lines.

PROFESSOR PICKUP

In Spain, in July 1936 . . .

THOMAS THE CYNIC

In Spain there was no *coup d'état* by a political party. It was a case of military sedition abetted by the intervention of foreign powers.

MR. DOUBLE YOU

I agree with you. The Spanish example lies outside the theme of our talk. Never mind the volunteers; that was a little war between regular armies. Still, who can guarantee that in other countries the *coup d'état* will go off as smoothly as it did in Italy and Germany?

THOMAS THE CYNIC

You're right; there is always an unforeseen element in every undertaking. Knowing this, Mussolini hesitated until the last minute. When he decided to use the threat of arms, he took the proper precautions for his own safety in case of failure. He didn't conceive of the March on Rome as an anticonstitutional move. Italo Balbo tells in his *Diary* about the meeting of Fascist leaders on October 16, 1922, at which the march on the capital was decided on. Its aim was defined as being "to force the government to resign and to drive the Crown to form a Fascist cabinet." In this way the illegal aspect of the operation was reduced to a minimum. At that meeting Mussolini asked the others if they thought Fascism's military forces were in a condition to march on Rome. General De Bono and General De Vecchi said no, and nobody confuted their arguments. In spite of this, it was decided to march on Rome anyway, but the reasons for the decision were entirely political. "If we don't attempt the *coup* at once," Balbo declared, "by spring it will be too late." And indeed there was no time to lose. Only by seizing the government could Fascism retain the support of its followers.

National Socialism acted in similar circumstances. If we look at the successful *coups* of the last decades, they all seem to take place at the peak of a curve. The fascist party, having reached its maximum power, seems to be hesitating as to what to do, and is finally forced to declare itself in a hurry just as the first signs of the descending curve become apparent. The expert politician can be judged by the speed with which he recognizes those decisive moments and by the aplomb with which he adapts himself to their requirements. Mussolini's hesitation was caused by his uncertainty about the King's attitude, which in turn would determine the behavior of the army's general staff. When Mussolini's guarantees to respect the constitution didn't seem sufficient, General Badoglio declared, "Five minutes of shooting and Fascism will collapse." There was no bragging in that statement. Mussolini was the first to be convinced of it. "We don't believe that General Badoglio's sinister intentions will come to anything," he wrote in his newspaper. "The regular army will not march against the blackshirts, simply because the Fascists will never march against the regular army, for which they feel the highest respect and infinite admiration." So every means was employed to win the King's sympathy for the Fascist cause, and the results were encouraging. On October 24, in the instructions drawn up in Naples for the March, which was to begin four days later, it was laid down that "if armed resistance on the part of the government is encountered, clashes with the troops are to be avoided and feelings of friendship and respect must be shown towards them." Some regiments were commanded by Fascist officers, but it was decided not to make use of them to avoid forcing officers loyal to the government to take reprisals. To win in an unarmed country, all Fascism needed was that the army remain neutral. Just in case, however, Mussolini appointed a secret military committee to lead the "insurrectional" movement. Not knowing how things were going to end, he wisely stayed off the committee himself. To direct operations, the committee set up headquarters in Perugia, while Mussolini stayed in Milan, an hour from the Swiss border.

MR. DOUBLE YOU

In America it would be difficult to organize a secret conspiracy. Not because of the police but because of newspaper reporters.

THOMAS THE CYNIC

The March on Rome was a very open secret; announcements were written on the walls of the city. Moreover, it's impossible to set masses in motion and keep it a secret. Even in serious insurrectional movements, the surprise element nowadays has been reduced to a minimum. An insurrection succeeds when the majority of the people expect it as something in-

evitable and necessary. Only the technical details of
the movement can and must be kept secret. Mussolini
never worried about this. A few weeks before the
March on Rome, he printed its geographical and stra-
tegical plan in his newspapers. In other words, the
idea of the March was in the air; everybody was talking about it. "When you want to attack the state, you
can't confine yourself to a little plot which is kept
more or less secret till the last moment," Mussolini
wrote at the end of September. "We have to give orders to hundreds of thousands of people, and it would
be an absurd hope, a presumption, to think of keeping
it a secret."

Shall I read you what Marx wrote about Louis
Bonaparte's *coup d'état?* "The *coup d'état* was Louis
Bonaparte's obsession. He had set foot on French soil
again with that idea. He was so gripped by it that he
was always mentioning it and discussing it. But he
was so weak that he kept dropping it again. The shadow
of the *coup d'état,* like a ghost, had become so familiar to the Parisians that when it finally appeared in
flesh and blood, they could hardly believe it was true.
So it wasn't the close-mouthed secrecy of the leader
of the Society of the 10th of December nor the sudden upheaval of the National Assembly that allowed
the *coup d'état* to succeed. It succeeded despite
indiscretions and lack of surprise, it was the necessary
and inevitable result of preceding developments."

PROFESSOR PICKUP

In Rome we saw a film on the March of the Fascist Legions toward the capital on March 28, 1922. To
tell you the truth, it made a profound impression on
us.

THOMAS THE CYNIC

You are Americans and you can believe in the movies? The reality was far more modest. The Fascist military plan developed in three directions: in the industrial cities of Turin, Milan, Genoa and Trieste, as well as in southern Italy, the Fascist squads stayed on the defensive; in central Italy and throughout the Po valley the Fascists seized local power without encountering any resistance, helped in fact by the military authorities and the police; and from these last-named regions, three columns were sent off with the assignment to make camp at a certain distance from Rome. They numbered about fourteen thousand, of whom only a part were armed with rifles and revolvers. These columns had no machine guns, no artillery or airplanes. They didn't even have tents or provisions. A couple of bomber planes would have been enough to decimate them and put them to flight. Instead, the greatest hardship suffered by those brave men was the rain. The few communications that the leaders of the three columns managed to exchange (and which were later published) speak only of rain. One of these leaders, Igliori, wrote to Bottai, the colleague nearest to him, that since he couldn't stay out in the open country in the rain, he was forced to go into Rome to keep his men out of the wet. Bottai (who was sheltered) answered, telling Igliori, to be patient and not to enter Rome prematurely and upset the political discussions then in progress between the King and the representatives of Fascism. On October 30 Mussolini, summoned by the King, left Milan for Rome in a sleeping car. That same evening the more soaked of the Fascist squads were allowed to enter the outlying suburbs of Rome to dry their clothes and get something to eat. The next day the news that Mussolini had been named Prime Minister spread through the whole country, and finally the Fascist squads began to hasten toward the capital, even from the most remote provinces, to parade past the Duce, the King and the newsreel cameramen.

PROFESSOR PICKUP

Yes, to the eyes of contemporaries historic events often seem petty. There are events that reveal their nobility only when they are seen in the perspective of centuries. How do you suppose the military critics of the period judged Joshua's occupation of Jericho? Their opinion was probably unflattering. But it has been handed down to us as a miracle. For seven times around the walls of the besieged city the trumpets of seven priests chosen by Joshua were sounded. When this liturgical rite had been performed, Joshua ordered his soldiers: "Let out war cries." And, at those shouts, the walls that girded the city fell down. The city was immediately invaded and sacked. The only person to be spared was the prostitute Rahab, because she had lodged Joshua's messengers in secret.

THOMAS THE CYNIC

In the Fascist *coup d'état* Madame Rahab's generous role was played by Parliament.

14.

Concerning the significance of consent by plebiscite, the reciprocal penetration of state and party, and the intensive raising of scapegoats.

MR. DOUBLE YOU

Mr. Cynic, this time let me furnish data for a change. A year before Nazism came to power, in the presidential elections of April 10, 1932, Hitler lost, with thirteen million votes to a good nineteen million given to Hindenburg. Even in the elections of March 1933 the Nazi party received only 43.8 per cent of the votes. Can you tell me what happened to those millions who voted against Nazism?

THOMAS THE CYNIC

A minority of them are now in concentration camps, in exile, or self-condemned to what is known as spiritual emigration, which means noncollaboration with the regime and retirement to private life. But the majority of them have climbed on to the bandwagon.

MR. DOUBLE YOU

How do you explain the behavior of that majority?

THOMAS THE CYNIC

I see you want to have fun today by asking me rhetorical questions. Don't you know that power easily creates consent? And moreover, those masses had been trained by their democratic leaders to obey without argument.

MR. DOUBLE YOU

That's a good one. Are you suggesting that political leaders should train their followers to think for themselves? Why should they act against their own interests? Anyway, all that the masses are fit for is to obey. It's a fiction to use them as an excuse for the number of different political parties. Political divisions reach the masses from outside. In fact, as the totalitarian countries show, the masses can do without political parties perfectly well.

PROFESSOR PICKUP

The problem is simple—Bernard Shaw told us that when we met him in Stresa, where he was vacationing. You merely have to turn your back on the little minorities of party men: liberals, republicans, syndicalists, socialists, Bolsheviks, anarchists, freethinkers, etc. Ignoring them, you organize the vast majority: people who would never dream of conspiring against the established order, who go to church or temple every week dressed in their finest, or play golf or tennis in elegant sports clothes, people who flock to coronations and royal marriages and military parades, drive five miles to see a dead monarch lying in state, who think they have a credo and a code, though in actual fact they merely do what everyone else does and are shocked by anyone who doesn't, who use their minds to do crossword puzzles or play bridge, and so on. This is a new version of Periander's advice to Trasibulus that he should cut down those stalks that grew higher than the others. If you remove the factious party machines, you restore the masses to their natural unity. This is the first task of every dictatorship.

THOMAS THE CYNIC

Don't delude yourselves, however, that you'll be able to restrict the use of force to the early period of the dictatorship and to the destruction of hostile organizations. Differences of opinion, differences of interest, are not always artificially created. To retain the people's support or, at any rate to maintain discipline, the terror must be lasting. That Bernard Shaw of yours, who claims to be a Labourite and distributes his admiration equally among Mussolini, Stalin and Pilsudski, is an intellectual libertine who knows very little about these things.

PROFESSOR PICKUP

Kindly stop quibbling. The difference between support given out of inner conviction and support won by force is merely technical and doesn't bear examination. We discussed this subject at length with the Fascist philosopher Giovanni Gentile, whom we met in Rome. The distinction between moral and material force, he said, is ingenuous. All force is ultimately moral force because, whatever its origin, its aim is always to subjugate the will. Whichever argument the leader adopts, sermon or cudgel, the result will be identical: the individual citizen is influenced and persuaded to give his support. As to what the convincing argument should be, whether sermon or cudgel, the matter is not one for abstract discussion. Replacing one political regime with another is like demolishing one building and then, with the old bricks, constructing another. The blows of the pick-axe will be inevitable.

THOMAS THE CYNIC

Still, you should be careful. It's unwise for the

neo-dictator to display too bold a face. It's useful, even for a dictatorship, to make a show of legitimacy, and nowadays the only acceptable claims to legitimacy are based on the will of the people. It's a falsehood, I agree, but the totalitarian dictatorship can't forego it. Indeed, it's one of the essential characteristics which distinguish modern dictatorships from the absolutist regimes of the past. The neo-dictator will therefore leave to his philosophers the task of finding an ethical rehabilitation for his beatings-up, and he will devote himself to disguising as sincere and spontaneous the consent extorted by terror. After he has killed or gagged his opponents, the modern dictator must proclaim his regime to be a superior form of democracy, the only genuine democracy, in fact—direct democracy. For this purpose he will organize daily mass rallies, and every now and then a plebiscite. This is an inevitable toll he must pay to the principles of his opponents, but it's nothing to worry about. Even for the opposition, in the final analysis, these were only slogans; these little inconsistencies don't shock anyone.

PROFESSOR PICKUP

Still that nonchalant attitude toward ideology can be dangerous. Is there no way of avoiding it? In the dispute between Boniface VIII and Philip the Fair, John of Paris pronounced the famous formula: *Populo faciente et Deo inspirante*. That seems to me a motto worth reviving.

MR. DOUBLE YOU

Frankly, gentlemen, all this idle gossip of yours is boring me. The will of the people is almost as mysterious a concept as God. The essential thing is to be able to maneuver the mechanism which can manufacture that will. If the Austrian plebiscite last spring had been called by Schuschnigg, it would surely have resulted in a majority favoring the independence of Austria. Since it was called by Hitler, it ended with a majority for union with Germany. Just suppose for a moment that the election machine in Russia could be maneuvered by Trotsky instead of Stalin. The man who today is an exile in Mexico would have the party and the country unanimously behind him, and would have to give severe instructions to prevent the "free elections" from expressing even more than one-hundred per cent unanimity.

THOMAS THE CYNIC

I suppose you know that there are countries where the government gets defeated in the elections without the world coming to an end?

MR. DOUBLE YOU

Defeated by whom? By the opposing machine, not by the masses. Who chooses the candidates? Who pays for the campaign?

PROFESSOR PICKUP

Aristotle criticized the way judges were elected in Crete; the system was based on the amount of applause that followed the proposal of each candidate's name in the assembly. He also criticized the fact that to be a candidate in Sparta a man had to take part in the frequent public banquets and pay for his own meal, which was beyond the means of many. What admirable simplicity! Applause and banquets are just as important in modern democracies as they were in Aristotle's time, but they're not mentioned in political treatises.

MR. DOUBLE YOU

Why do you have to keep dragging those Greeks into it? In the earliest period of American democracy, the electorate was officially directed by Congress, which nominated special congressional committees or legislative caucuses to choose and present the candidates. In 1825 the task of "making" the elections was given over to the free initiative of the people; this seemed progress, but instead it was decadence. A new kind of histrionic demagogue sprang up. Elections became expensive affairs, maneuvered by professional politicians without principles or programs, who forced themselves on public opinion as trusts monopolize the market. It can't be said that freedom and public morality have gained anything in the process. Of the two systems, the old one is surely the simpler.

PROFESSOR PICKUP

That's what justifies our motto: *Back to Grass Roots.*

THOMAS THE CYNIC

It's certainly an inspiring slogan. The return to grass roots suggests a pioneering spirit, a healthy, innocent landscape, the happy recollections of a golden age. Moreover it has an obviously traditionalist and noble sense. "Back to grass roots" is a magnificent and evasive answer to every problem, even those whose origins are unknown or perhaps still to come.

MR. DOUBLE YOU

As to whether I should go back to the system of the congressional or legislative caucus, there's of course no harm in discussing it right away; but I wouldn't want to put the cart before the horse. First I'd like to see how things turn out for me, and then I can begin to think about caucuses.

THOMAS THE CYNIC

That's the wisest suggestion I've heard in the course of our conversations. What matters to the neo-dictator isn't nearly so much the institutional form of power as the fact of having that power at his sole and entire disposal. In other words, he prefers which-ever form will allow him the most unconfined and un-assailable hold on power. You can find confirmation of this in the history of every dictatorship. What may sometimes seem uncertainty or inconsistency is in-stead the sign of prudent empiricism. But the most in-structive example in the matter of choosing institu-tions is given us by Lenin, who possessed, to a perhaps insuperable degree, a concrete sense of power, to-gether with an unscrupulousness that knew no limit. In 1917 he began by saying he was prepared to accept the results of the Constituent Assembly, but he re-tracted this as soon as he saw that he was in the mi-nority. He dismissed the Assembly with violence, set-ting up against it the slogan: "All power to the Soviets." But when he realized that he couldn't suc-ceed in driving the Mensheviks, the social-revolution-aries and the anarchists out of the Soviets, he liqui-dated the Soviets too, keeping only the name as a façade to conceal the barefaced hegemony of his party.

PROFESSOR PICKUP

That's all very well, but behind him Lenin had a party which was both suited and equal to the task of taking over all the levers of public administration and making them work.

THOMAS THE CYNIC

No dictator has ever had trouble finding civil servants.

MR. DOUBLE YOU

At home we're way ahead of you on that score. Since the time of Andrew Jackson, it's the rule in our public life that there should be the "spoils of office." To the victor belong the spoils. The Civil Service Act of 1881 did try to put a brake on things, but even so the best-paying jobs, especially those in the Treasury and Post Office departments, are still an excellent prey for the toadies of the winner. Not to mention the various pork-barrel jobs in city government.

PROFESSOR PICKUP

When all the opposition parties and groups have been suppressed, it's obvious that the enforcement of the Civil Service Act—like every other limitation of power—will be left to the discretion of the winning party.

THOMAS THE CYNIC

Yes, but don't be so sure that a single-party system is going to be an Open Sesame. If you liquidate the organizations of your opponents, this act no doubt eliminates a certain number of your difficulties, but it also creates new ones which can be rather tiresome.

You must start with the principle that the dictatorship of a single party is literally nonsense. The moment one party uses force to suppress the others, it automatically puts an end to its own existence as a party. I hope you won't make the mistake of imagining that differences of opinion are an artificial product and that they will disappear with the abolition of opposition newspapers or the leveling of social classes. As long as men have the capacity to think, they will never be unanimous on all the problems of existence. So when other possibilities of expression are lacking, differences of interest and point of view will spring up within the single party, forming various trends and creating rivalries among the leaders themselves. What's the dictator to do? Permit argument? That would be ruinous. These differences must be repressed as attacks on the security of the state. The single party will have to be placed under constant control. This will justify modifications in the party structure. When the Communists gave up their basic formation, the traditional city or district groups, and instead established cells in offices, workshops, departments and blocks of flats, this move was made not only for reasons of efficiency but also for discipline. The cell-system makes it easy to track down and isolate even the slightest element of opposition.

In an authoritarian regime the structure of the single party is of prime importance. You can see this clearly if you look at any form of competition among kindred forces. The prevalence of the Jesuits over other Catholic orders, the victories of Marx over Bakunin in the First International, of Lenin over Martov in Russian Social Democracy, and of Stalin over Trotsky in Bolshevism, of Hitler over Ludendorff and the other rivals of the German Right—all these victories were vastly facilitated by organizational superiority. The most up-to-date totalitarian party will be the one that profits from the lessons of Saint Ignatius Loyola, Marx, Stalin and Hitler. Its organization will inevitably be hierarchical and will be based, not on committees or other collective bodies, but on the responsibility of single individuals. Bonaparte said, "Better one bad general than two good ones." Every chief will be named by his immediate superior. To prevent a leader from sinking roots in a given region and becoming popular there, he will be periodically transferred, preferably to a locality where he is completely unknown. In the local sections there will, of course, be no discussion—only work. The principal activity there will consist of helping people who come with everyday problems. Nothing will ever be decided at the meetings of a local section. Only the leaders may take decisions. The lower ranks of the party will have nothing to do with creating the party line; their sole task will be to follow it and propagandize it among the masses.

MR. DOUBLE YOU

You aren't trying to tell us that that's something exclusive to totalitarian parties? I happen to know from personal experience that the work of the lower ranks in a democratic party isn't very different. I served my political apprenticeship as a precinct leader in such a party. I don't want to brag, but I always managed to get at least two thirds of the votes in the block they assigned me. My uncle helped me and so did an Italian barber, who was really amazing in the art of convincing the reluctant ones. This barber wasn't a political thinker, mind you; in fact, he didn't understand a thing about politics. But he was funny. These poor people needed help, and I fixed up the ones I could as firemen, as janitors in public schools, or in other jobs of that sort. The ones I couldn't help I handed over to the Italian barber, who made them laugh. I had to work like a dog to become a ward leader with about thirty precincts under me. But even then I was never called to discuss the party's policies. I had a boss over me who ran the party machine the way he drove his Ford. If I had been patient, I could have waited for him to die, in the hope of taking over his job. But, in the first place, I wasn't that patient—he was as sound as a dollar—and, in the second place, he was only a cog in the wheel, a bigger cog than I was, but still only a cog.

THOMAS THE CYNIC

What you have been saying, Mr. Double You, was already on our list of the conditions that favor totalitarian ventures in our time. A question that we haven't yet gone into is whether, in a single-party regime, it's the State that absorbs the party or vice versa. Personally I would say that it happens both ways, through the person of the Leader and the group of his chief associates. The Leader runs the party and the State. He uses the State to keep the party submissive and the party to maintain political control of the State. Party discipline will be considered the dictatorship's most precious possession. Party officers will be subjected to intensive training.

PROFESSOR PICKUP

I have already worked out a complete project for our party training school.

MR. DOUBLE YOU

Is pantautology supposed to become our official doctrine? Before I say yes, I want to hear the opinion of other experts.

THOMAS THE CYNIC

Since it's not truth but efficiency that you're after, Mr. Double You, it hardly matters whether you adopt that ideology or another. In every age authoritarian regimes have taught the most fantastic doctrines and have had excellent results. Nowadays, with the forms that mass civilization is taking, the operation has become much easier. Since truth has ceased to be self-evident, and free inquiry is declared incompatible with public order, the persuasive power of the official ideology is ultimately based on the prestige of the police. The official ideology will therefore become fixed at a compulsory rate, like legal tender, and to reject that ideology will be a crime, like not recognizing the value assigned to the ruble or the dollar. It is indispensable, however, that the teaching be dogmatic, leaving not the slightest room for doubt. Doubt: that's your enemy.

PROFESSOR PICKUP

Yes, but we unluckily have a class of professors, artists and writers. They who are particularly untrustworthy. They are so conceited, they'll do anything just to be different, and they'll swallow any crackpot notion provided it comes from abroad.

THOMAS THE CYNIC

In the case of those who, as you say, are fundamentally vain, it shouldn't be hard to win them over by exploiting their weak point, lavishing awards and laurel crowns on them, installing them in university chairs and state sinecures. Bear in mind that an exclusive intellectual activity is liable to deform the normal mental equilibrium and lead to narcissism. There are very few artists or intellectuals who altogether escape this professional disease. Since in this inevitable solitude the narcissist is filled with rancor against society, to receive a tribute from the new Chief of State would be bound to have a tremendous effect on him. As a general rule the intellectual or artist is instinctively pleased with anything that will add to his fame and loathes whatever is likely to harm it. His private concept of good and evil is based on these considerations. At all events, any lingering doubts he may have will vanish as soon as he gets wind of the danger that the exalted tribute in question might go to some colleague instead of to him.

PROFESSOR PICKUP

Bismarck said once that poets and prostitutes can always be had for money.

THOMAS THE CYNIC

Money, with the people we're talking about, isn't always the most effective means. Flattery is far superior. And it mightn't be a bad idea if you paid a little homage to some famous foreign writer or artist too. You needn't fear they'll snub you; their reputation for being inaccessible is almost always a fraud. They love to see their photographs in foreign newspapers. And after all, who wouldn't appreciate a free stay in a big luxury hotel, with a good cuisine and choice cellar? You needn't be afraid of wasting money; all this would greatly enhance the prestige of the new regime, because these famous writers now exert a fascination over the masses that goes far beyond the merely esthetic. With the decline of the churches, the role of spiritual mentor has fallen to these gentlemen. Are you afraid there may be some black sheep among them who are not to be won over by bribes or flattery? You can denounce them to the police, with the order that they are to be treated as hardened criminals.

MR. DOUBLE YOU

I wouldn't say that in our country the influence of the churches is declining. On the contrary. And an extra inconvenience is that we have so many different kinds of them.

THOMAS THE CYNIC

That's a drawback that can be turned into an advantage if the dictatorship is clever enough to exploit their rivalries. Churchmen, like the gods, love those on whom fortune shines. Their civil obedience, to whatever power, is solidly based on the belief that all authority comes from God, and on the counsel to render unto Caesar the things that are Caesar's. In short, these people are well-disposed. On the other hand, the boundary between the divine and the human isn't so clearly drawn that they don't sometimes also give to Caesar the things that are God's, or claim for God some things that are Caesar's. These confusions mustn't shock you. The neo-dictator will appreciate the advantage of being declared the Man of Providence and of having a prayer inserted in the liturgy beseeching divine protection for his person.

MR. DOUBLE YOU

I don't believe in the next world.

THOMAS THE CYNIC

Neither does Mussolini, but religious approval smoothed the way for his triumph in the referendum he called after the conciliation with the Vatican.

PROFESSOR PICKUP

When it comes to handling priests, he has certainly been cleverer than Hitler. And yet, in Germany too, both Catholic and Protestant clergy were quite ready to collaborate.

MR. DOUBLE YOU

It looks as though Hitler scorned the line of least resistance.

THOMAS THE CYNIC

That's more or less true of all dictatorships. Montesquieu defined the dictator as "he who chops down a tree to pick an apple."

MR. DOUBLE YOU

Not so much for the apple itself, I think, as to display his strength. There are absent-minded people who need a frequent demonstration of strength as a reminder.

THOMAS THE CYNIC

In its first period every dictatorship goes through an inevitable phase of adjustment and organization. It's a huge task; the whole of society has to come under the control of the party-state. No margin will be left for spontaneity or for the initiative of intermediary powers, of groups or of private individuals. Not only the functioning of labor unions and managerial associations, but even such activities as artistic creation, leisure and amusement will take place under the surveillance of the party-state. A tight network of party officers will control every citizen. In places of work and of rest, on trains and buses, in the home, the individual citizen must feel the watchful eye of authority upon him. The party officer combines the functions of spy, social worker and hotel detective. What could be more private, you might think, than the love-making of a married couple? Mussolini has worked out ways of influencing even that. Italian bachelors have to pay a special tax. Contraceptive devices have been outlawed and druggists are forbidden to sell them. Prolific mothers receive a cash prize and an autographed photograph of the Duce.

MR. DOUBLE YOU

I wonder if you are not putting too many irons in the fire. How can a political party take on all these nuisances?

THOMAS THE CYNIC

Obviously the party that planned and carried out the *coup d'état* could never do it. And that's why that party has to be purged and reformed from top to bottom. After eliminating his opponents the neo-dictator will find that his greatest difficulties come from the very men who helped him most in his struggle for power. He will save himself on condition that he acts promptly and ruthlessly with them.

MR. DOUBLE YOU

It's true that Mussolini, Hitler and Stalin all had to deal with that painful job. But do you think it can be generalized?

THOMAS THE CYNIC

Definitely. In the first place, remember that the capacities required for preparing and carrying out a *coup d'état* are very different from those required for administrating power. But there is more to it than that. Party seniority will create in some men the presumptuous notion that they have merits and rights independently of the Leader's benevolence. They may feel they have been neglected in the division of the spoils. There will be others who took the slogans of the conspiratorial period seriously; they won't approve when they see the Leader disowning those same slogans, or even preaching the contrary once he has got into power. Finally, the most dangerous men of all will be those who enjoy wide popularity and lose no opportunities to increase it. All these people must be watched and eliminated. The precedents you have just mentioned offer a wide choice of methods. In some cases arrest or deportation will be enough; in others, it will have to be assassination by unknown enemies, or else trial before a special court on the charge of conspiracy, treason, corruption, and so on. Not least of the advantages to be derived from this purge of his own ranks are the praises that will be heaped on the neo-dictator by many of his former opponents who will discern in him that rarest of all statesmanlike qualities—the unhesitating capacity to sacrifice even one's friends for the welfare of the nation. At the same time the neo-dictator must draw new men into his ranks, men endowed with the qualities needed by a ruling party, men who will be docile, conformist, blindly devoted, if not actually imbecile.

MR. DOUBLE YOU

Don't say anything against imbeciles, please. Personally, I've always had a weakness for them. The owner of a large factory confided in me that the most profitable part of his plant was one where all the workers came from a school for simple-minded boys. Unfortunately science hasn't yet discovered a sure way of increasing cretinism.

THOMAS THE CYNIC

You're both really hard to please. You have the radio, the movies, the yellow press, sport—what more do you want? Of course the whole secret is to use them with intelligence.

PROFESSOR PICKUP

The best propaganda is still public works. You can't deny that Hitler has achieved wonderful things in that line, and Mussolini too.

THOMAS THE CYNIC

I know, the Italian trains now run on time. It's an old story; from the Pharaohs to Stalin, all tyrants have achieved wonderful things. But wonders aren't enough to prove the tyrants were right.

MR. DOUBLE YOU

What does being right have to do with it? The religion of our time is efficiency. Under Hitler's guidance, the German economy has absorbed the millions of unemployed he inherited from the Weimar Republic. What more do you want?

PROFESSOR PICKUP

Hitler's done better than that. He has turned the tables on traditional socialism, taking away its symbols, calling his own party National Socialism, using the color red for his banners, and making the first of May a national holiday.

THOMAS THE CYNIC

Yes, you're right. The deathblow to any opposition is to outlaw it and then appropriate its program. After that there's nothing left of it. In 1917 Lenin used those tactics successfully against his dangerous rivals, the revolutionary socialists. They had the peasants on their side, and for the proletarian revolution promoted by the Bolsheviks there was no greater menace than an autonomous movement of agricultural workers. The goal of eliminating the revolutionary socialists was pursued through a well-timed coordination of terrorist police activity, with the adoption of the rival party's own agrarian program. It was in this connection that Lenin promulgated his famous decree confiscating the great landholdings for the benefit of local agrarian committees and the peasants' regional soviets. Later, of course, when they no longer had any rural opposition, the Bolsheviks went back to their original agrarian policy, considering the peasants as second-class citizens and exploiting them to the advantage of the industrialization program. This masterly example was followed by Stalin in his struggle against Trotsky. First he accused his rival of industrialist deviationism; then, having exiled him, Stalin hastened to adopt the industrialization program. When, in cases of ideological or political incompatibility, the neo-dictator doesn't dare go that far, he should attempt it in words, at least, or in some symbolic manner. There is no more economical or innocuous device for solving problems than to change their names. Similarly, under Italian Fascism, the rights and privileges of the capitalists were in fact strengthened, while in the Charter of Labor promulgated by the regime capitalism was defined as outmoded. It was simply renamed "corporativism," following the example of the monk who, in deference to the rules of fasting, ate beefsteaks only after he had baptized them as codfish.

MR. DOUBLE YOU

You make it all sound much too easy. If all changes were only a matter of words, don't you think that dictatorships would have fewer opponents?

PROFESSOR PICKUP

To me, dictatorship seems the right medicine for every diseased society.

THOMAS THE CYNIC

Perhaps dictatorship should be compared not so much to a medical cure as to an orthopedic apparatus.

MR. DOUBLE YOU

Why not? I have the highest respect for orthopedics. Of all branches of medicine, it seems the most honest to me.

THOMAS THE CYNIC

But the problems remain. The political defeat of

the socialist parties doesn't eliminate the concrete problems of production and social organization that the socialists were trying to solve. Nor does it destroy the working class, which in modern countries constitutes the majority of the population, and whose interests have for many decades been defended and represented by the socialist movement. The originality of fascism, in comparison to earlier reactionary movements, is that it fights the revolution with the revolution's own methods, appropriating its symbols, its techniques, its tactics, all its externals—but without solving its problems. Instead of solutions, fascism offers palliatives: obligatory organization, social welfare, paid vacations, mother-and-child care. Similarly the plebiscite is an ersatz for democracy, and the cult of Fatherland or race makes up for the lack of a real faith.

MR. DOUBLE YOU

You mustn't criticize ersatz products if they're a necessity. If an indispensable product is lacking, you have to find some kind of substitute. At times the substitute article is of better quality and more useful than the real thing.

PROFESSOR PICKUP

And besides, what is all this mania for solving problems? Society isn't a problem; it's a reality and all one can do is accept it.

MR. DOUBLE YOU

Let's not stray from the point. The biggest problems for any regime derive from the fact that it has to run the country. When a regime has had to improvise the higher echelons of its administration practically overnight, how can it protect itself against stupidity, waste, sabotage and corruption? Not to mention natural calamities like droughts, floods, epidemics, which inevitably have social consequences.

THOMAS THE CYNIC

Dictatorships have a genuine panacea for ills of every kind: the prompt sacrifice of appropriate scapegoats. The method is quick and has none of the defects of the democratic method, with its scandals, its interminable wrangling in parliament, its investigating committees that discover nothing, and its trials that last for decades. Besides, to sacrifice scapegoats creates the illusion that the public administration is severely controlled. It satisfies not only the need for justice but also the less noble and more widespread need for vengeance. So I can safely state that a large supply of scapegoats, assorted and suitable for every conceivable occasion, is indispensable to the security of the authoritarian state, quite as indispensable as the raising of cattle to the prosperity of agriculture.

PROFESSOR PICKUP

You're surely not thinking of a preordained list of candidates for sacrifice?

THOMAS THE CYNIC

No, that would involve unjust and unsuitable exclusions, whereas you might say that—excepting only the Leader—this fate could befall any citizen. Of course there are certain categories of individuals who by virtue of this very tradition are, even from before birth, predestined for sacrifice—Jews, Negroes, anarchists, foreigners, for instance. But the astute dictator, when the moment is ripe, will be able to derive a double advantage from the scapegoat ritual by choosing for sacrifice, as guilty of some national disaster, the people toward whom he bears some ancient grudge. There are, however, also painful cases in which reasons of state may force him to deprive himself of his best friends and collaborators. This course may be recommended whenever rumors begin to circulate that the dictator himself is responsible for some national catastrophe.

PROFESSOR PICKUP

You needn't think that it would cost Mr. Double You any great effort to sacrifice his best friends.

MR. DOUBLE YOU

Certainly less than to sacrifice myself.

THOMAS THE CYNIC

It is to be hoped that the friends chosen will be worthy of the high honor and that, when they are sent before the court which is to sentence them to the electric chair, they will confess their guilt convincingly.

PROFESSOR PICKUP

Suppose they refuse? Suppose they proclaim their innocence?

THOMAS THE CYNIC

Then they prove that they are dyed-in-the-wool traitors and doubly deserving of an ignoble death. In any case, it's not very difficult in a dictatorship to fabricate apocryphal confessions and corroborate them with plausible documents and witnesses.

MR. DOUBLE YOU

Can you explain the "spontaneous" confessions of the defendants in the great Moscow trials during these last years?

THOMAS THE CYNIC

I don't think there can be any explanation of those trials apart from the explanation of present-day Russian reality as a whole. I mean that even if we knew the technique which led those defendants spontaneously to confess nonexistent crimes, it wouldn't be easy to apply the technique elsewhere and achieve the same terrifying results. A run-of-the-mill *coup d'état* obviously wouldn't be enough. There are certain masterpieces of the juridical art that only a genuine revolution, which has been inspired by an irresistible impulse of idealism, can produce. But don't be discouraged, Mr. Double You; what can't be repeated can at least be imitated. The raw materials are different, but the aim is identical. A shrewd and systematic exploitation of scapegoats should, moreover, reinforce the Leader's prestige. Among so many scoundrels he is the only one who never makes a mistake. All the evils of the regime are blamed on his collaborators; all the good is laid at his door. Thus grows the legend of the Good Tyrant, whose influence spreads far beyond his own party. In Russia there were anti-Bolsheviks who were careful not to include Lenin in their opposition; and it seems that in Italy there are pro-Mussolini anti-Fascists.

MR. DOUBLE YOU

Why are you so sarcastic when you talk about the dictator's popularity? I imagine him as being much closer to the people than any of the traditional statesmen are.

PROFESSOR PICKUP

Yes, in fact the silence of the opposition parties makes it easier for him to hear the faintest murmur of complaint. In Rome they showed us the famous "Mouth of Truth," where in ancient times citizens could place anonymous denunciations. Mussolini, for his part, has recognized the legitimacy of the *jus murmurandi*. And as everyone knows, Stalin periodically organizes campaigns of Communist self-criticism.

THOMAS THE CYNIC

With a very definite boundary line, however. The denunciations and criticisms allowed can concern only marginal events, marginal people, marginal circumstances of public life. Never general policy, and still less the person of the Leader.

PROFESSOR PICKUP

Whatever his personal defects may be, the Leader's function must be sacred and above all discussion. It is the party's duty to foster the cult of his person. No expedient should be neglected that might help to create around the Leader an atmosphere of idolatry. This is the essential condition that gives him the power to ask citizens even for the sacrifice of their lives.

THOMAS THE CYNIC

Keeping the cult of the Leader going is the principal function of the press, radio and propaganda monopoly. To achieve its ends, it must be protected by the banning of hostile foreign books and newspapers and by the systematic disturbance of foreign radio broadcasts. In spite of all this, we know from experience that because of the strangeness of human nature, this monopoly cannot prevent sudden upheavals of public opinion, due to unpredictable causes. Have no illusions. When that happens, the safety of the regime must be entrusted to another monopoly—that of arms. Nine tenths of the citizens hate me, Cromwell said, but what do I care, as long as one tenth is armed? Still, it's obvious that even totalitarian dictatorships cannot be eternal.

MR. DOUBLE YOU

What can defeat them, if their opponents are defenseless and movements of opinion impotent?

THOMAS THE CYNIC

That's a question to which experience has not yet given an answer. Totalitarianism is a recent phenomenon, barely at the beginning of its development. For the moment nothing seems to indicate any decline in the conditions that favor it. We may wonder whether today's mass civilization will not perhaps end by losing its negative characteristics, and in a long historical perspective, by reaction from the excess of state-worship, a libertarian humanism may not be born. But these are abstract conjectures.

PROFESSOR PICKUP

It is less abstract to remark that the *coup d'état*, even when carried out to preserve or restore the old social order, tends to create a new order.

THOMAS THE CYNIC

I doubt that it has the time. If I may venture the comparison, totalitarian regimes are attracted to war like iron to a magnet. And I don't think any dictatorship can survive a military defeat.

MR. DOUBLE YOU

Surely you don't mean to assert that modern war trains the masses for self-government?

THOMAS THE CYNIC

I wouldn't dare go that far.

MR. DOUBLE YOU

Then you mean that certain forms of totalitarianism can be followed by other forms?

THOMAS THE CYNIC

I don't think it's inevitable, but it's probable. Thus Nazism will be able to give communism back the masses it had received as a present earlier on. Or vice versa. And in the competition for power, there is nothing to prevent a totalitarian party from giving itself a democratic label. The transformation won't cost more than the price of new uniforms and the change of symbols; and even that, as is only proper, will be taken care of by the treasury.

MR. DOUBLE YOU

Don't you think that a situation of economic prosperity, together with a few brilliant successes in international relations might enable a dictatorship to give up terror and democratize itself, so to speak?

THOMAS THE CYNIC

Alexis de Tocqueville has already warned that dictatorships run their greatest risks not when they tighten the reins, but when they loosen them. It is difficult then to stop the long-repressed centrifugal motion and prevent it from turning into a catastrophe.

PROFESSOR PICKUP

Our last meeting, Mr. Cynic, is coming to an end. Mr. Double You's doctors tell him he can leave again. But before we say good-bye, I'd like to ask you a personal question. If, as you seem to think, the great trend of our epoch, thanks to mass civilization, is towards totalitarianism of one kind or another, why are you so opposed to all of them?

THOMAS THE CYNIC

I don't believe that the honest man is forced to submit to history.

PROFESSOR PICKUP

Ye Gods, did anyone ever hear a more blasphemous notion?

MR. DOUBLE YOU

Mr. Cynic, your visits have made my stay in this city much less dreary than it promised to be. I want to thank you. If luck is with me, may I hope to have you in America as my guest?

THOMAS THE CYNIC

Why not? But it would be dangerous for both of us. I would undoubtedly join your opponents in order to fight you, and if you follow the advice I've given you, you'll send me to jail.

Ignazio Silone

Ignazio Silone was born May 1, 1900, at Pescina, a small and ancient Central Italian town that lies on the slopes leading to the Maiella mountains. The country and its people, for centuries isolated by their hills from the surrounding culture, have remained central to his life and work. His maturity was hurried by a combination of natural disaster (the 1915 earthquake in which fifty thousand people died in seconds), poverty and the casual, cynical oppression by authority of the peasants among whom he lived. His political activity forced him into exile from Mussolini's Italy, and from 1930 until the fall of the Fascist government he lived and worked in Davos, Switzerland. Here he began to write the famous books—Fontamara, Bread and Wine, The School for Dictators, The Seed Beneath the Snow—*that made him a distinguished and distinctive figure in world literature. After the war he returned to Italy and now he lives in Rome.*